30
THINGS
I NEED TO TELL
MY WIFE

FAMILY
Christian Stores·

The quoted ideas expressed in this book (but not scripture verses) are not, in all cases, exact quotations, as some have been edited for clarity and brevity. In all cases, the author has attempted to maintain the speaker's original intent. In some cases, quoted material for this book was obtained from secondary sources, primarily print media. While every effort was made to ensure the accuracy of these sources, the accuracy cannot be guaranteed. For additions, deletions, corrections or clarifications in future editions of this text, please write FAMILY CHRISTIAN STORES.

Cover Design by Kim Russell / Wahoo Designs
Page Layout by Bart Dawson

ISBN 978-1-60587-053-3

Printed in the United States of America

... A MESSAGE FOR COUPLES

30
THINGS
I NEED TO TELL
MY WIFE

TABLE OF CONTENTS

Introduction —7

What Every Husband Should Say to His Wife:

1. "I Love You Now and Forever." —9

2. "I Will Honor You by Putting God First in My Life." —15

3. "I Understand the Importance of Cooperation." —22

4. "I Am Totally Committed to Our Marriage." —29

5. "I Will Always Try to Focus on the Positive." —35

6. "Thank You for Encouraging Me. I Will Always Try to Encourage You." —42

7. "Thank You for Sharing My Hopes and Dreams." —49

8. "I Want to Hear What You Have to Say." —56

9. "Thank You for Your Forgiveness. I Will Always Forgive You, Too." —62

10. "The Example We Set Is Important. Thank You for Being an Example of All That Is Good." —69

11. "I Treasure Our Family." —76

12. "I Will Always Honor Our Marriage and Be Faithful to You." —82

13. "We Are Richly Blessed. I Thank God for Our Marriage and Our Family." —88

14. "Thank You for Your Patience. I Will Be Patient with You, Too." —95

15. "I Celebrate Your Love, and I Celebrate Our Marriage." —102

16. "Thank You for Being Faithful When Times Are Tough." —109

17. "Time Here on Earth Is Short and Precious. I Want to Spend as Much of It with You as I Can." —116

18. "Thank You for Your Integrity. It Enriches Our Marriage." —122

19. "You Always Bring Me Joy." —129

20. "You Bring Such Joy and Happiness to Our Marriage. I Am so Grateful that God Brought Us Together." —135

21. "You Are Beautiful in Every Way." —142

22. "I Praise God for You and for Our Marriage." —148

23. "I Will Never Stop Loving You." —155

24. "I Understand that We Are on a Spiritual Journey." —162

25. "I Know That Life Is Short, so I Treasure the Time We Spend Together." —169

26. "I Understand the Importance of Clear, Loving, Open Lines of Communication." —176

27. "I Thank You for Your Prayers, and I Will Never Stop Praying for You." —182

28. "You Are My Best Friend." —189

29. "I Thank God for Our Marriage." —195

30. "Our Love Will Last Forever." —202

INTRODUCTION

"But the greatest of these is love"—seven familiar words that remind us of a simple truth: God places a high priority on love . . . and so should we. Faith is important, of course. So, too, is hope. But love is more important still.

Considering all the wonderful things your wife has done for you, you may have a few things to say to her. You may want to express your love, your thanks, your praise, or your faithfulness. And if you'd like to communicate these things and more, then the ideas in this book can help.

This text contains 30 things that every husband (and that includes you) needs to tell his wife. If you sincerely wish to make your marriage flourish, take these ideas, put them into your own words, and express them to your bride. And while you're at it, please remember that it isn't enough to simply talk about these principles; you must also weave them into the fabric of your marriage. When you do, you'll learn firsthand the truth of God's Word: "the greatest of these" is now—and will forever be—the love that is shared between you and your wife.

1

What Every Husband Should Say to His Wife:

"I LOVE YOU NOW AND FOREVER."

Now these three remain: faith, hope, and love.
But the greatest of these is love.
1 Corinthians 13:13 HCSB

As a thoughtful husband, you understand the crucial role that love does play—and should play—in every marriage, including your own. And the familiar words of 1st Corinthians 13 serve as a beautiful reminder of the importance and the power of love. Yet sometimes, amid the inevitable struggles of everyday life, you may lose sight—at least temporarily—of the love you feel for your wife.

Christ showed His love for us on the cross, and, as Christians we are called to return Christ's love by sharing it. And Paul instructed husbands to love their wives in the same way that Christ loved His church: "Husbands, love your wives, just as also Christ loved the church and gave Himself for her" (Ephesians 5:25 HCSB).

Sometimes, of course, love is easy (puppies and sleeping children come to mind), and sometimes love is hard (imperfect husbands and wives come to mind). But God's Word is clear: We are to love our wives (and everyone for that matter) at all times, not just when they seem most lovable.

So do the right thing: Tell your wife that you love her every chance you get. Tell her in person; call her on the phone; leave her notes; give her encouragement, cooperation, and praise. Demonstrate your love with words and deeds—your wife needs both . . . and she deserves both.

MORE FROM GOD'S WORD ABOUT LOVE

Above all, keep your love for one another at full strength, since love covers a multitude of sins.

1 Peter 4:8 HCSB

If I speak the languages of men and of angels, but do not have love, I am a sounding gong or a clanging cymbal.

1 Corinthians 13:1 HCSB

Love one another earnestly from a pure heart.

1 Peter 1:22 HCSB

Now the goal of our instruction is love from a pure heart, a good conscience, and a sincere faith.

1 Timothy 1:5 HCSB

The one who does not love does not know God, because God is love.

1 John 4:8 HCSB

MORE GREAT IDEAS . . .

Marriage should be many hours of joy interrupted by an occasional minute or two of frustration—not the other way around.

Marie T. Freeman

The first natural tie of human society is man and wife.

St. Augustine

Joy is love exalted; peace is love in repose; gentleness is love in society; goodness is love in action; faith is love on the battlefield; meekness is love in school; and temperance is love in training.

D. L. Moody

Only a love that has no regard for vessels and jars—appearances or image—only a love that will lavish its most treasured essence on the feet of Jesus can produce the kind of fragrance that draws cynics and believers alike into His presence.

Gloria Gaither

Line by line, moment by moment, special times are etched into our memories in the permanent ink of everlasting love in our relationships.

Gloria Gaither

Love is an attribute of God. To love others is evidence of a genuine faith.

Kay Arthur

Suppose that I understand the Bible. And, suppose that I am the greatest preacher who ever lived! The Apostle Paul wrote that unless I have love, "I am nothing."

Billy Graham

Affection should be the underlying atmosphere of marriage twenty-four hours a day, seven days a week.

Ed Young

A TIP FOR HUSBANDS

You should only say "I love you" on the days that end in "y."

YOUR OWN IDEAS ABOUT . . .
Ways to Express the Love You Feel for Your Wife

‑ Giving her time to relax when
she needs it.

‑ Helping her with the Daily jobs that
need to be done, both around the
house and outside it.

‑ Being there for her when she
needs to talk

Dear Aubrey
I love you very much, and
want to spend the rest
of my life with you. I
know at times this statement
will be tested, I believe that
having it written down though
will help us to remember why we
love each other

2

What Every Husband Should Say to His Wife:

"I WILL HONOR YOU BY PUTTING GOD FIRST IN MY LIFE."

You shall have no other gods before Me.

Exodus 20:3 NKJV

Do you and your wife put God first in your marriage? Or do you allow yourselves to be hijacked by the inevitable obligations and distractions of 21st-Century life? When you and your beloved allow Christ to reign over your lives and your marriage, your household will be eternally blessed.

God loved this world so much that He sent His Son to save it. And now only one real question remains: what will you and yours do in response to God's love? The answer should be obvious: You must put God first in every aspect of your lives, including your marriage.

God is with you always, listening to your thoughts and prayers, watching over your every move. As the demands of everyday life weigh down upon you, you may be tempted to ignore God's presence or—worse yet—to rebel against His commandments. But, when you quiet yourself and acknowledge His presence, God touches your heart and restores your spirits.

At this very moment, God is seeking to work in you and through you. So why not let Him do it right now?

MORE FROM GOD'S WORD ABOUT PUTTING GOD FIRST

Be careful not to forget the Lord.

Deuteronomy 6:12 HCSB

It is good to give thanks to the Lord, and to sing praises to Your name, O Most High; to declare Your lovingkindness in the morning, and Your faithfulness every night.

Psalm 92:1-2 NKJV

Love the Lord your God with all your heart, with all your soul, and with all your strength.

Deuteronomy 6:5 HCSB

The Devil said to Him, "I will give You their splendor and all this authority, because it has been given over to me, and I can give it to anyone I want. If You, then, will worship me, all will be Yours." And Jesus answered him, "It is written: You shall worship the Lord your God, and Him alone you shall serve."

Luke 4:6-8 HCSB

For where your treasure is, there your heart will be also.

Luke 12:34 HCSB

17

MORE FROM GOD'S WORD ABOUT FEAR OF GOD

Don't consider yourself to be wise; fear the Lord and turn away from evil.

Proverbs 3:7 HCSB

The fear of the Lord is the beginning of knowledge, but fools despise wisdom and instruction.

Proverbs 1:7 NKJV

To fear the Lord is to hate evil.

Proverbs 8:13 HCSB

The fear of the Lord is the beginning of wisdom, and the knowledge of the Holy One is understanding.

Proverbs 9:10 HCSB

The fear of the Lord is the beginning of wisdom; all who follow His instructions have good insight.

Psalm 111:10 HCSB

MORE GREAT IDEAS . . .

If God has the power to create and sustain the universe, He is more than able to sustain your marriage and your ministry, your faith and your finances, your hope and your health.

Anne Graham Lotz

Love has its source in God, for love is the very essence of His being.

Kay Arthur

It is when we come to the Lord in our nothingness, our powerlessness and our helplessness that He then enables us to love in a way which, without Him, would be absolutely impossible.

Elisabeth Elliot

Marriage is God's idea. He "crafted" it. If your marriage is broken, all the "repairmen" or counselors or seminars you take it to will be unable to fix it; take it to Him. The Creator who made it in the first place can make it work again.

Anne Graham Lotz

When I have learnt to love God better than my earthly dearest, I shall love my earthly dearest better than I do now. When first things are put first, second things are not suppressed but increased.

C. S. Lewis

Oh, that we might discern the will of God, surrender to His calling, resign the masses of activities, and do a few things well. What a legacy that would be for our children.

Beth Moore

The love life of the Christian is a crucial battleground. There, if nowhere else, it will be determined who is Lord: the world, the self, and the devil—or the Lord Christ.

Elisabeth Elliot

A TIP FOR HUSBANDS

Today, spend time talking to your wife about the role that God does play—and should play—in your marriage.

YOUR OWN IDEAS ABOUT . . .
Ways to Put God First in Your Marriage.

3

What Every Husband Should Say to His Wife:

"I UNDERSTAND THE IMPORTANCE OF COOPERATION."

If a kingdom is divided against itself,
that kingdom cannot stand.
If a house is divided against itself,
that house cannot stand.
Mark 3:24-25 HCSB

Have you and your wife learned the fine art of cooperation? And do you tell your wife every day that you're ready, willing, and able to help her get things done? If so, you have learned the wisdom of "give and take," not the foolishness of "me first."

Cooperation is the art of compromising on little things while keeping your eye on the big thing: your relationship.

Cooperative relationships grow and flourish over time. But, when couples fail to cooperate, they unintentionally sow seeds of dissatisfaction and disharmony.

If you're like most of us, you're probably a little bit headstrong: you probably want most things done in a fashion resembling the popular song "My Way." But, if you are observant, you will notice that those people who always insist upon "my way or the highway" usually end up with "the highway."

A better strategy for all concerned is to abandon the search for "my way" and search instead for "our way." That tune has a far happier ending. So today, tell your wife that you're serious about being a cooperative, solution-oriented husband, a man who's fully prepared to do his fair share, and then some. She needs to hear those words from you. Now.

More from God's Word About Cooperation

Blessed are the peacemakers . . . .

Matthew 5:9 HCSB

And with many other words he testified and strongly urged them, saying, "Be saved from this corrupt generation!"

Acts 2:40 HCSB

Carry one another's burdens; in this way you will fulfill the law of Christ.

Galatians 6:2 HCSB

Pursue peace with everyone, and holiness—without it no one will see the Lord.

Hebrews 12:14 HCSB

Two are better than one because they have a good reward for their efforts. For if either falls, his companion can lift him up; but pity the one who falls without another to lift him up.

Ecclesiastes 4:9-10 HCSB

MORE FROM GOD'S WORD ABOUT HELPING OTHERS

When we have the opportunity to help anyone, we should do it. But we should give special attention to those who are in the family of believers.

Galatians 6:10 NCV

You address me as "Teacher" and "Master," and rightly so. That is what I am. So if I, the Master and Teacher, washed your feet, you must now wash each other's feet. I've laid down a pattern for you. What I've done, you do.

John 13:15 MSG

Then a Samaritan traveling down the road came to where the hurt man was. When he saw the man, he felt very sorry for him. The Samaritan went to him, poured olive oil and wine on his wounds, and bandaged them. Then he put the hurt man on his own donkey and took him to an inn where he cared for him.

Luke 10:33-34 NCV

The one who blesses others is abundantly blessed; those who help others are helped.

Proverbs 11:25 MSG

More Great Ideas . . .

In the bond of marriage, we are to stand at the altar of Sacrifice or we're not to stand at all.

Beth Moore

Being committed to one's mate is not a matter of demanding rights, but a matter of releasing rights.

Charles Swindoll

There is nothing wrong with a marriage that sacrifice wouldn't heal.

Elisabeth Elliot

Selfishness and marriage don't mix.

Marie T. Freeman

Husbands and wives who live happily ever after learn to give and take and to reach agreement by mutual consent. A man or woman with an unmovable backbone is in real trouble. God made backbones that can stand rigid but can also bend when necessary.

Vance Havner

A Christian wife's responsibility balances delicately between knowing when to submit and when to outwit. Adapting to our husbands never implies the annihilation of our creativity, rather the blossoming of it.

Ruth Bell Graham

There is no such thing as a no-maintenance marriage, but energy and time devoted to this holy enterprise will reap lasting, valuable dividends every time.

Ed Young

Cooperation is a two-way street, but for too many couples, it's the road less traveled.

Marie T. Freeman

A TIP FOR HUSBANDS

Be cooperative. Remember that the two of you are in this thing together, so play like teammates, not rivals.

YOUR OWN IDEAS ABOUT . . .

The Importance of Cooperation Within Your Marriage.

_____

_____

_____

_____

_____

_____

_____

_____

_____

_____

_____

_____

_____

_____

_____

_____

_____

_____

4

What Every Husband Should Say to His Wife:

"I AM TOTALLY COMMITTED TO OUR MARRIAGE."

So they are no longer two, but one flesh.
Therefore what God has joined together,
man must not separate.

Matthew 19:6 HCSB

In a good marriage, the words "love" and "commitment" are intertwined. According to God, genuine love is patient, unselfish, and kind, but it's goes beyond that—genuine love is committed love, and that means that genuine love is more than a feeling . . . it is a decision to make love endure, no matter what.

Unfortunately, we live in a world where marriage vows are sometimes taken far too lightly. Too many couples are far too quick to push the panic button—or the eject button—and the results are predictably tragic.

As a married man who has vowed to love your wife "till death do you part," you must take that vow very seriously. Your wife must know, beyond any doubt, that you are totally committed to her, totally committed to your family, and totally committed to your marriage. How can you do it? The best place to start is by putting God right where He belongs: at the absolute center of your family and your marriage.

When you and your spouse worship God together, you'll soon notice a change in your relationship. When the two of you sincerely embrace God's love, you will feel differently about yourself, your marriage, your family, and your world. When you and your spouse embrace God's love together, your marriage will be transformed. And, when the two of you accept the Father's grace and share His love, you will be blessed here on earth and throughout eternity.

So, if you genuinely seek to build a marriage that will stand the test of time, make God the foundation. When you do, your love will endure for a lifetime and beyond.

MORE FROM GOD'S WORD ABOUT COMMITMENT

To sum up, each one of you is to love his wife as himself, and the wife is to respect her husband.

Ephesians 5:33 HCSB

A man leaves his father and mother and bonds with his wife, and they become one flesh.

Genesis 2:24 HCSB

A husband should fulfill his marital duty to his wife, and likewise a wife to her husband.

1 Corinthians 7:3 HCSB

Wives, be submissive to your husbands, as is fitting in the Lord. Husbands, love your wives and don't become bitter against them.

Colossians 3:18-19 HCSB

MORE GREAT IDEAS . . .

Being committed to one's mate is not a matter of demanding rights, but a matter of releasing rights.

Charles Swindoll

There is nothing wrong with a marriage that sacrifice wouldn't heal.

Elisabeth Elliot

If a husband and wife are deeply committed to Jesus Christ, they enjoy enormous advantages over the family with no spiritual dimension.

James Dobson

A beautiful relationship with your mate will enhance your creativity and upgrade your standard of living while improving your quality of life.

Zig Ziglar

They [Billy and Ruth Graham] not only share a deep love for one another, but a mutual respect.

Gigi Graham Tchividjian

The institution of marriage has been a sacred bond of fidelity between a man and a woman in every culture throughout recorded history. The pledge of loyalty and mutual support represented by marriage vows is a promise of commitment that extends to every aspect of life.

James Dobson

How committed are you to breaking the ice of prayerlessness so that you and your mate can seek the Lord openly and honestly together, releasing control over your marriage into the capable, trustworthy, but often surprising hands of God?

Stormie Omartian

A TIP FOR HUSBANDS

Commitment first! The best marriages are built upon an unwavering commitment to God and an unwavering commitment to your wife. So, if you're totally committed, congratulations; if you're not, you're building your marriage (and your life) on a very shaky foundation.

YOUR OWN IDEAS ABOUT . . .
The Importance of Commitment Within Your Marriage.

_____

_____

_____

_____

_____

_____

_____

_____

_____

_____

_____

_____

_____

_____

_____

_____

_____

_____

5

What Every Husband Should Say to His Wife:

"I Will Always Try to Focus on the Positive."

Finally brothers, whatever is true, whatever is honorable, whatever is just, whatever is pure, whatever is lovely, whatever is commendable—if there is any moral excellence and if there is any praise—dwell on these things.

Philippians 4:8 HCSB

A Christian marriage should be cause for celebration, but sometimes we don't feel much like celebrating. In fact, when the weight of the world seems to bear down upon our shoulders, celebration may be the last thing on our minds . . . but it shouldn't be. As God's children, we are all blessed beyond measure on good days and bad. This day is a non-renewable resource— once it's gone, it's gone forever. We should give thanks for this day while using it for the glory of God.

What will your attitude be today? Will you be fearful, angry, bored, or worried? Will you infect your marriage with the twin blights of cynicism and negativity? Or will you choose to be a better man, a man who decides, instead, to celebrate your life and your loved ones? The choice is yours, and so are the consequences.

Please remember that God has richly blessed you, and He wants you to rejoice in His gifts. But, He will not force His joy upon you; you must claim it for yourself.

So today, and every day hereafter, celebrate the life that God has given you. Think optimistically about yourself, your marriage, your family, and your future. Look for goodness, not faults; look for strengths, not shortcomings. And vow to be a positive influence on everybody you meet, starting with your bride. She deserves that kind of husband. And you deserve the rewards that inevitably come to men (like you) who learn how to count—and how to keep counting—their blessings.

MORE FROM GOD'S WORD ABOUT ATTITUDE

Make your own attitude that of Christ Jesus.

Philippians 2:5 HCSB

For the word of God is living and powerful, and sharper than any two-edged sword, piercing even to the division of soul and spirit, and of joints and marrow, and is a discerner of the thoughts and intents of the heart.

Hebrews 4:12 NKJV

Let this mind be in you which was also in Christ Jesus, who, being in the form of God, did not consider it robbery to be equal with God, but made Himself of no reputation, taking the form of a bondservant, and coming in the likeness of men. And being found in appearance as a man, He humbled Himself and became obedient to the point of death, even the death of the cross.

Philippians 2:5-8 NKJV

Set your minds on what is above, not on what is on the earth.

Colossians 3:2 HCSB

More from God's Word About Optimism

Make me hear joy and gladness.

Psalm 51:8 NKJV

For God has not given us a spirit of fearfulness, but one of power, love, and sound judgment.

2 Timothy 1:7 HCSB

My cup runs over. Surely goodness and mercy shall follow me all the days of my life; and I will dwell in the house of the Lord Forever.

Psalm 23:5-6 NKJV

I am able to do all things through Him who strengthens me.

Philippians 4:13 HCSB

But if we hope for what we do not see, we eagerly wait for it with patience.

Romans 8:25 HCSB

MORE GREAT IDEAS . . .

Attitude is more important than the past, than education, than money, than circumstances, than what people do or say. It is more important than appearance, giftedness, or skill.

Charles Swindoll

A little rain can strengthen a flower stem. A little love can change a life.

Max Lucado

A positive attitude will have positive results because attitudes are contagious.

Zig Ziglar

Life goes on. Keep on smiling and the whole world smiles with you.

Dennis Swanberg

All things being equal, attitude wins. All things not being equal, attitude sometimes still wins.

John Maxwell

What you see and hear depends a good deal on where you are standing; it also depends on what sort of person you are.

C. S. Lewis

Some people complain that God put thorns on roses, while others praise Him for putting roses on thorns.

Anonymous

Developing a positive attitude means working continually to find what is uplifting and encouraging.

Barbara Johnson

A TIP FOR HUSBANDS

Today, spend time thinking about the impact that your attitude has upon your wife and upon the rest of your family.

YOUR OWN IDEAS ABOUT . . .

The Importance of Maintaining a Positive Attitude.

_____

_____

_____

_____

_____

_____

_____

_____

_____

_____

_____

_____

_____

_____

_____

_____

_____

_____

6

"THANK YOU FOR ENCOURAGING ME. I WILL ALWAYS TRY TO ENCOURAGE YOU."

Therefore encourage one another and build each other up
as you are already doing.

1 Thessalonians 5:11 HCSB

Marriage is a team sport, and all of us need occasional pats on the back from our teammate. In the Book of Proverbs, we read that, "A word aptly spoken is like apples of gold in settings of silver" (25:11 NIV). This verse reminds us that the words we speak can and should be beautiful offerings to those we love.

All of us have the power to enrich the lives of our loved ones. Sometimes, when we feel uplifted and secure, we find it easy to speak words of encouragement and hope. Other times, when we are discouraged or tired, we can scarcely summon the energy to uplift ourselves, much less anyone else. But, as loving Christians, our obligation is clear: we must always measure our words carefully as we use them to benefit others and to glorify our Father in heaven.

God intends that we speak words of kindness, wisdom, and truth, no matter our circumstances, no matter our emotions. When we do, we share a priceless gift with our loved ones, and we give glory to the One who gave His life for us. As believers, we must do no less.

More from God's Word About Encouragement

I want their hearts to be encouraged and joined together in love, so that they may have all the riches of assured understanding, and have the knowledge of God's mystery—Christ.

Colossians 2:2 HCSB

Two are better than one because they have a good reward for their efforts. For if either falls, his companion can lift him up; but pity the one who falls without another to lift him up.

Ecclesiastes 4:9-10 HCSB

Carry one another's burdens; in this way you will fulfill the law of Christ.

Galatians 6:2 HCSB

And let us be concerned about one another in order to promote love and good works.

Hebrews 10:24 HCSB

Finally, all of you be of one mind, having compassion for one another; love as brothers, be tenderhearted, be courteous.

1 Peter 3:8 NKJV

MORE FROM GOD'S WORD ABOUT CRITICISM

Don't speak evil against each other, my dear brothers and sisters. If you criticize each other and condemn each other, then you are criticizing and condemning God's law. But you are not a judge who can decide whether the law is right or wrong. Your job is to obey it.

James 4:11 NLT

Our Father is kind; you be kind. Don't pick on people, jump on their failures, criticize their faults—unless, of course, you want the same treatment. Don't condemn those who are down; that hardness can boomerang. Be easy on people; you'll find life a lot easier.

Luke 6:36-37 MSG

A man who lacks judgment derides his neighbor, but a man of understanding holds his tongue.

Proverbs 11:12 NIV

So let's agree to use all our energy in getting along with each other. Help others with encouraging words; don't drag them down by finding fault.

Romans 14:19-20 MSG

MORE GREAT IDEAS . . .

We have the Lord, but He Himself has recognized that we need the touch of a human hand. He Himself came down and lived among us as a man. We cannot see Him now, but blessed be the tie that binds human hearts in Christian love.

Vance Havner

Praise and recognition from the one you love will definitely enhance the performance of any individual, male or female.

Zig Ziglar

I can usually sense that a leading is from the Holy Spirit when it calls me to humble myself, to serve somebody, to encourage somebody, or to give something away. Very rarely will the evil one lead us to do those kind of things.

Bill Hybels

Sometimes one little spark of kindness is all it takes to reignite the light of hope in a heart that's blinded by pain.

Barbara Johnson

The truest help we can render an afflicted man is not to take his burden from him, but to call out his best energy, that he may be able to bear the burden himself.

Phillips Brooks

One of the ways God refills us after failure is through the blessing of Christian fellowship. Just experiencing the joy of simple activities shared with other children of God can have a healing effect on us.

Anne Graham Lotz

In each of my friends there is something that only some other friend can fully bring out. By myself I am not large enough to call the whole man into activity; I want other lights than my own to show all his facets.

C. S. Lewis

A TIP FOR HUSBANDS

Be encouraging. You should be your wife's biggest booster, not her constant critic.

YOUR OWN IDEAS ABOUT . . .
Simple Ways You Can Encourage Your Wife

_____

_____

_____

_____

_____

_____

_____

_____

_____

_____

_____

_____

_____

_____

_____

_____

_____

7

"THANK YOU
FOR SHARING MY HOPES
AND DREAMS."

*Now may the God of hope fill you with all joy
and peace in believing, so that you may overflow
with hope by the power of the Holy Spirit.*
Romans 15:13 HCSB

Do you and your wife spend time together planning for the future and sharing your dreams? And, are you willing to entertain the possibility that God has big plans in store for your marriage? Hopefully so. Yet sometimes, especially if you've recently experienced a life-altering disappointment, you may find it difficult to envision a brighter future for yourself or your family. If so, it's time to reconsider your own capabilities . . . and God's.

Your Heavenly Father created you and your loved ones with unique gifts and untapped talents; your job is to tap them. When you do, you'll begin to feel an increasing sense of confidence in yourself and in your future.

It takes courage to dream big dreams and even more courage to share them. You will discover that kind of courage when you do three things: accept the past, trust God to handle the future, and make the most of the time He has given you today. Nothing is too difficult for God, and no dreams are too big for Him—not even yours. So start living—and dreaming—accordingly.

Dreams are wonderful things to share with your wife. Have you shared yours lately? Hopefully so. But if you've been hesitant to give voice to your hopes and plans, remember this: dreaming works best when it's a team sport.

MORE FROM GOD'S WORD ABOUT HOPEFUL DREAMS

Be of good courage, and he shall strengthen your heart, all ye that hope in the LORD.

Psalm 31:24 KJV

Therefore, as we have opportunity, we must work for the good of all, especially for those who belong to the household of faith.

Galatians 6:10 HCSB

But as it is written: What no eye has seen and no ear has heard, and what has never come into a man's heart, is what God has prepared for those who love Him.

1 Corinthians 2:9 HCSB

Looking at them, Jesus said, "With men it is impossible, but not with God, because all things are possible with God."

Mark 10:27 HCSB

But I will hope continually and will praise You more and more.

Psalm 71:14 HCSB

MORE FROM GOD'S WORD ABOUT HOPE

Let us hold on to the confession of our hope without wavering, for He who promised is faithful.

Hebrews 10:23 HCSB

For I know the thoughts that I think toward you, says the Lord, thoughts of peace and not of evil, to give you a future and a hope. Then you will call upon Me and go and pray to Me, and I will listen to you.

Jeremiah 29:11-12 NKJV

Hope deferred makes the heart sick.

Proverbs 13:12 NKJV

Sustain me as You promised, and I will live; do not let me be ashamed of my hope.

Psalm 119:116 HCSB

We have this hope—like a sure and firm anchor of the soul—that enters the inner sanctuary behind the curtain.

Hebrews 6:19 HCSB

MORE GREAT IDEAS . . .

Love is the seed of all hope. It is the enticement to trust, to risk, to try, and to go on.

Gloria Gaither

You cannot out-dream God.

John Eldredge

To make your dream come true, you have to stay awake.

Dennis Swanberg

The future lies all before us. Shall it only be a slight advance upon what we usually do? Ought it not to be a bound, a leap forward to altitudes of endeavor and success undreamed of before?

Annie Armstrong

Sometimes our dreams were so big that it took two people to dream them.

Marie T. Freeman

Always stay connected to people and seek out things that bring you joy. Dream with abandon. Pray confidently.

Barbara Johnson

Set goals so big that unless God helps you, you will be a miserable failure.

Bill Bright

Do we reach for nothing in life because our reaching opens us up to tragedy?

John Eldredge

A Tip for Husbands

Today, think about the importance of sharing your hopes and dreams with your wife. And then, get busy sharing.

YOUR OWN IDEAS ABOUT . . .
Your Dreams You Should Share with Your Wife.

_____

_____

_____

_____

_____

_____

_____

_____

_____

_____

_____

_____

_____

_____

_____

_____

_____

8

"I WANT TO HEAR WHAT YOU HAVE TO SAY."

*My dearly loved brothers, understand this:
everyone must be quick to hear,
slow to speak, and slow to anger.*

James 1:19 HCSB

What a blessing it is when our loved ones genuinely seek to understand who we are and what we think. Just as we wish to be understood by others, so, too, should we seek to understand the hopes and dreams of our spouses and our family members.

Are you in the habit of listening to your wife? Do you listen carefully (not superficially), and do you take time to think about the things she says? If so, you're building a stronger marriage. But if you allow the obligations of everyday living to interfere with the communications you share with your mate, it's time to reorder your priorities.

You live in a busy world, a place where it is all too easy to overlook the needs of others, but God's Word instructs you to do otherwise. In the Gospel of Matthew, Jesus declares, "In everything, therefore, treat people the same way you want them to treat you, for this is the Law and the Prophets" (Matthew 7:12 NASB). This is the Golden Rule, and it should govern your marriage.

Do you want your voice to be heard? Of course you do. So, in adherence with the Golden Rule, you should also let your wife's voice be heard, too—heard by you.

More from God's Word About Listening

A wise man will hear and increase learning.

Proverbs 1:5 NKJV

A fool's way is right in his own eyes, but whoever listens to counsel is wise.

Proverbs 12:15 HCSB

Listen to counsel and receive instruction so that you may be wise in later life.

Proverbs 19:20 HCSB

Let your graciousness be known to everyone. The Lord is near.

Philippians 4:5 HCSB

The one who is from God listens to God's words. This is why you don't listen, because you are not from God.

John 8:47 HCSB

MORE GREAT IDEAS . . .

The cliché is true: People don't care what we know until they know we care.

Rick Warren

One of the best ways to encourage someone who's hurting is with your ears—by listening.

Barbara Johnson

The first service one owes to others in the fellowship consists in listening to them. Just as love of God begins in listening to His Word, so the beginning of love for the brethren is learning to listen to them. It is God's love for us that He not only gives us His Word but lends us His ear. So it is His work that we do for our brother when we learn to listen to him.

Dietrich Bonhoeffer

In the soul-searching of our lives, we are to stay quiet so we can hear Him say all that He wants to say to us in our hearts.

Charles Swindoll

An essential condition of listening to God is that the mind should not be distracted by thoughts of resentment, ill-temper, hatred or vengeance, all of which are comprised in the general term, the wrath of man.

R. V. G. Tasker

Listening is loving.

Zig Ziglar

When we come to Jesus stripped of pretensions, with a needy spirit, ready to listen, He meets us at the point of need.

Catherine Marshall

A Tip for Husbands

It's hard to listen before you speak, but it's worth it. It takes conscious effort to hold your tongue until your ears are fully engaged. When you are able to do so, your efforts will usually be rewarded.

YOUR OWN IDEAS ABOUT . . .
Ways You Can Become a Better Listener.

_____

_____

_____

_____

_____

_____

_____

_____

_____

_____

_____

_____

_____

_____

_____

_____

9

What Every Husband Should Say to His Wife:

"THANK YOU FOR YOUR FORGIVENESS. I WILL ALWAYS FORGIVE YOU, TOO."

All bitterness, anger and wrath, insult and slander must be removed from you, along with all wickedness. And be kind and compassionate to one another, forgiving one another, just as God also forgave you in Christ.

Ephesians 4:31-32 HCSB

If you want to make your love last a lifetime, you and your wife you must learn the art of forgiveness. Why? Because all of our loved ones are imperfect (as are we). How often must we forgive each other? More times than we can count. In other words, we must not just learn how to forgive; we must learn how to keep forgiving (Matthew 18:21-22).

Perhaps granting forgiveness is hard for you. If so, you are not alone. Granting heartfelt forgiveness is often difficult for hardheaded husbands—difficult but not impossible.

When it comes to the hard work of forgiving those who have injured us, God is willing to help, but He expects us to do some of the work—and when we do so, we are blessed.

When we learn the art of forgiveness, we earn peace within our marriages and peace within our hearts. But when we harbor bitterness against others, we forfeit that peace—and by doing so, we bring needless harm to ourselves and to our loved ones. So, if there exists even one person, alive or dead, whom you have not forgiven (and that includes yourself or your wife), follow God's commandment—forgive. Because bitterness, anger, and regret are emotions that have no place in your life or your marriage.

More from God's Word About Forgiveness

Hatred stirs up conflicts, but love covers all offenses.

Proverbs 10:12 HCSB

A person's insight gives him patience, and his virtue is to overlook an offense.

Proverbs 19:11 HCSB

Be merciful, just as your Father also is merciful.

Luke 6:36 HCSB

And whenever you stand praying, if you have anything against anyone, forgive him, so that your Father in heaven may also forgive you your wrongdoing.

Mark 11:25 HCSB

May mercy, peace, and love be multiplied to you.

Jude 1:2 HCSB

MORE FROM GOD'S WORD ABOUT STAYING ANGRY

Don't let your spirit rush to be angry, for anger abides in the heart of fools.

Ecclesiastes 7:9 HCSB

My dearly loved brothers, understand this: everyone must be quick to hear, slow to speak, and slow to anger, for man's anger does not accomplish God's righteousness.

James 1:19-20 HCSB

A fool's displeasure is known at once, but whoever ignores an insult is sensible.

Proverbs 12:16 HCSB

All bitterness, anger and wrath, insult and slander must be removed from you, along with all wickedness. And be kind and compassionate to one another, forgiving one another, just as God also forgave you in Christ.

Ephesians 4:31-32 HCSB

A gentle answer turns away anger, but a harsh word stirs up wrath.

Proverbs 15:1 HCSB

MORE GREAT IDEAS . . .

God calls upon the loved not just to love but to be loving. God calls upon the forgiven not just to forgive but to be forgiving.

Beth Moore

Forgiveness is actually the best revenge because it not only sets us free from the person we forgive, but it frees us to move into all that God has in store for us.

Stormie Omartian

We are products of our past, but we don't have to be prisoners of it. God specializes in giving people a fresh start.

Rick Warren

Only the truly forgiven are truly forgiving.

C. S. Lewis

Miracles broke the physical laws of the universe; forgiveness broke the moral rules.

Philip Yancey

After the forgiving comes laughter, a deeper love—and further opportunities to forgive.

Ruth Bell Graham

The sequence of forgiveness and then repentance, rather than repentance and then forgiveness, is crucial for understanding the gospel of grace.

Brennan Manning

Forgiveness is the precondition of love.

Catherine Marshall

A TIP FOR HUSBANDS

When your wife becomes angry or upset, you'll tend to become angry and upset, too. Resist that temptation. Keep your cool, even when everybody else is losing theirs! By not fanning the flames, you'll help extinguish the fire.

YOUR OWN IDEAS ABOUT . . .
The Importance of Forgiveness.

10

"THE EXAMPLE WE SET IS IMPORTANT. THANK YOU FOR BEING AN EXAMPLE OF ALL THAT IS GOOD."

*Be an example to the believers in word, in conduct,
in love, in spirit, in faith, in purity.*
1 Timothy 4:12 NKJV

Whether you and your wife realize it or not, your marriage serves as a powerful example to family and friends. So here's the big question: what kind of example is your marriage? Is yours a marriage that honors God? Is it a marriage that strengthens the bonds of family? Is it a marriage that others should seek to emulate? If so, you are fortunate, you are wise, and you are blessed.

We live in a cynical, temptation-filled world where negative role models abound and positive role models are often in short supply. That's why your positive role model is so important. When you and your wife serve as positive examples for other couples, you are helping those couples visualize positive changes that they can make in their own marriages.

Phillips Brooks advised, "Be such a person, and live such a life, that if every person were such as you, and every life a life like yours, this earth would be God's Paradise." And that's sound advice because our families and friends are watching . . . and so is God.

MORE FROM GOD'S WORD ABOUT BEING AN EXAMPLE

Set an example of good works yourself, with integrity and dignity in your teaching.

Titus 2:7 HCSB

Do all things without complaining and disputing, that you may become blameless and harmless, children of God without fault in the midst of a crooked and perverse generation, among whom you shine as lights in the world.

Philippians 2:14-15 NKJV

You are the light of the world. A city that is set on a hill cannot be hidden. Let your light so shine before men, that they may see your good works and glorify your Father in heaven.

Matthew 5:14, 16 NKJV

Now then, we are ambassadors for Christ, as though God were pleading through us: we implore you on Christ's behalf, be reconciled to God.

2 Corinthians 5:20 NKJV

More from God's Word About Obeying God

Those who obey his commands live in him, and he in them. And this is how we know that he lives in us: We know it by the Spirit he gave us.

1 John 3:24 NIV

You shall walk after the Lord your God and fear Him, and keep His commandments and obey His voice, and you shall serve Him and hold fast to Him.

Deuteronomy 13:4 NKJV

When all has been heard, the conclusion of the matter is: fear God and keep His commands.

Ecclesiastes 12:13 HCSB

If they obey and serve him, they will spend the rest of their days in prosperity and their years in contentment.

Job 36:11 NIV

For it is not those who hear the law who are righteous in God's sight, but it is those who obey the law who will be declared righteous.

Romans 2:13 NIV

MORE GREAT IDEAS . . .

Integrity of heart is indispensable.

John Calvin

If I take care of my character, my reputation will take care of itself.

D. L. Moody

There is no way to grow a saint overnight. Character, like the oak tree, does not spring up like a mushroom.

Vance Havner

Your light is the truth of the Gospel message itself as well as your witness as to who Jesus is and what He has done for you. Don't hide it.

Anne Graham Lotz

You can never separate a leader's actions from his character.

John Maxwell

Are you willing to follow the light—are you willing to be the light?

Criswell Freeman

More depends on my walk than my talk.

D. L. Moody

Among the most joyful people I have known have been some who seem to have had no human reason for joy. The sweet fragrance of Christ has shown through their lives.

Elisabeth Elliot

A Tip for Husbands

Your marriage, in a very real sense, is a sermon. What kind of sermon will you and your wife choose to preach? As you think about this question, remember that the words you choose to speak may have some impact on others, but not nearly as much impact as the lives you choose to live.

YOUR OWN IDEAS ABOUT . . .
Ways That You and Your Wife Set a Positive Example
for Others to Follow.

_____

_____

_____

_____

_____

_____

_____

_____

_____

_____

_____

_____

_____

_____

_____

_____

_____

_____

11

What Every Husband Should Say to His Wife:

"I TREASURE OUR FAMILY."

Choose for yourselves today the one you will worship . . . .
As for me and my family, we will worship the Lord.
Joshua 24:15 HCSB

As a thoughtful husband, you know that your family is a priceless treasure from God. And if you're a wise husband, you'll make certain that your wife knows that you know. How? By telling her how thankful you are for the gift of family, that's how.

But sometimes, you'll be tempted to rush through life while giving little notice to your blessings. After all, if you're a busy husband working in a demanding world, the pressures can be intense. As those pressures build, you may tend to focus so intently upon your obligations to your family that you forget to give thanks for your family. But to do so is a big mistake. So even when the demands of everyday life are great, you must never forget that you have been entrusted with a profound responsibility: the responsibility of contributing to your family's emotional and spiritual well-being. It's a big job, but with God's help, you're up to the task.

When you place God squarely in the center of your family's life—when you worship Him, praise Him, trust Him, and love Him—then He will most certainly bless you and yours in ways that you could have scarcely imagined.

So the next time your family life becomes a little stressful, remember this: That little band of men, women, kids, and babies is a priceless treasure on temporary loan from the Father above. And it's your responsibility to praise God for that gift—and to act accordingly.

More from God's Word About Family

If a kingdom is divided against itself, that kingdom cannot stand. If a house is divided against itself, that house cannot stand.

Mark 3:24-25 HCSB

The one who brings ruin on his household will inherit the wind.

Proverbs 11:29 HCSB

Unless the Lord builds a house, its builders labor over it in vain; unless the Lord watches over a city, the watchman stays alert in vain.

Psalm 127:1 HSCB

Their first responsibility is to show godliness at home and repay their parents by taking care of them. This is something that pleases God very much.

1 Timothy 5:4 NLT

Love must be without hypocrisy. Detest evil; cling to what is good. Show family affection to one another with brotherly love. Outdo one another in showing honor.

Romans 12:9-10 HCSB

MORE GREAT IDEAS . . .

Homes that are built on anything other than love are bound to crumble.

Billy Graham

The only true source of meaning in life is found in love for God and his son Jesus Christ, and love for mankind, beginning with our own families.

James Dobson

There is so much compassion and understanding that is gained when we've experienced God's grace firsthand within our own families.

Lisa Whelchel

A home is a place where we find direction.

Gigi Graham Tchividjian

Calm and peaceful, the home should be the one place where people are certain they will be welcomed, received, protected, and loved.

Ed Young

Love is most often found in the home—in the presence of a caring and considerate mate who nurtures love daily.

Zig Ziglar

More than any other single factor in a person's formative years, family life forges character.

John Maxwell

Every Christian family ought to be, as it were, a little church, consecrated to Christ, and wholly influenced and governed by His rules.

Jonathan Edwards

A TIP FOR HUSBANDS

Today, think about the importance of saying "yes" to your family even if it means saying "no" to other obligations.

YOUR OWN IDEAS ABOUT . . .
God's Gift to You: Your Family.

_____

_____

_____

_____

_____

_____

_____

_____

_____

_____

_____

_____

_____

_____

_____

_____

_____

_____

12

What Every Husband Should Say to His Wife:

"I WILL ALWAYS HONOR OUR MARRIAGE AND BE FAITHFUL TO YOU."

Honor marriage, and guard the sacredness of sexual intimacy between wife and husband. God draws a firm line against casual and illicit sex.

Hebrews 13:4 MSG

The best relationships—and the best marriages—are built upon a foundation of honesty and trust. Without trust, marriages soon begin to wither; with trust, marriages soon begin to flourish.

For Christian men and women, honesty is the right policy because it's God's policy. God's Word makes it clear: "Lying lips are an abomination to the Lord, but those who deal truthfully are His delight" (Proverbs 12:22 NKJV).

Sometimes, honesty is difficult; sometimes, honesty is painful; sometimes, honesty makes us feel uncomfortable. Despite these temporary feelings of discomfort, we must make honesty the hallmark of all our relationships; otherwise, we invite needless suffering into our own lives and into the lives of those we love.

Do you want your love to last forever? Then you and your wife must build a marriage based upon mutual trust and unerring truth. Both of you deserve nothing less . . . and neither, for that matter, does God.

MORE FROM GOD'S WORD ABOUT TRUST

The one who lives with integrity lives securely, but whoever perverts his ways will be found out.

Proverbs 10:9 HCSB

Love must be without hypocrisy. Detest evil; cling to what is good. Show family affection to one another with brotherly love. Outdo one another in showing honor.

Romans 12:9-10 HCSB

The just man walketh in his integrity: his children are blessed after him.

Proverbs 20:7 KJV

The one who lives with integrity will be helped, but one who distorts right and wrong will suddenly fall.

Proverbs 28:18 HCSB

For the eyes of the Lord range throughout the earth to show Himself strong for those whose hearts are completely His.

2 Chronicles 16:9 HCSB

MORE GREAT IDEAS . . .

The greatest gift you can give your marriage partner is your fidelity. The greatest character trait you can provide your spouse and your family is moral and ethical self-control.

Charles Swindoll

Love is not soft as water is; it is solid as a rock on which the waves of hatred beat in vain.

Corrie ten Boom

Truth becomes hard if it is not softened by love, and love becomes soft if not strengthened by truth.

E. Stanley Jones

My commitment to my marriage vows places me in an utterly unique and profoundly significant relationship with the most important human being on earth—my spouse.

Joni Eareckson Tada

Blessed assurance, Jesus is mine! O what a foretaste of glory divine!

Fanny Crosby

Trust is like "money in the bank" in a marriage. There must be a reasonable amount of it on deposit to ensure the security of a marital union.

Ed Young

We sometimes fear to bring our troubles to God because we think they must seem small to Him. But, if they are large enough to vex and endanger our welfare, they are large enough to touch His heart of love.

R. A. Torrey

Would you rather trust a guy who wrote a book—or the One who wrote The Book?

Anonymous

A TIP FOR HUSBANDS

God can handle every challenge you and your wife face. You can trust Him to manage every aspect of your life, including your marriage.

YOUR OWN IDEAS ABOUT . . .
The Importance of Trust in Your Marriage.

_____

_____

_____

_____

_____

_____

_____

_____

_____

_____

_____

_____

_____

_____

_____

_____

_____

13

What Every Husband Should Say to His Wife:

"WE ARE RICHLY BLESSED. I THANK GOD FOR OUR MARRIAGE AND OUR FAMILY."

*I have come that they may have life,
and that they may have it more abundantly.*

John 10:10 NKJV

Christ came in order that we might have life abundant and life eternal. Eternal life is the priceless possession of all who invite Christ into their hearts, but God's abundance is optional: He does not force it upon us.

When we entrust our hearts and our days to the One who created us, we experience abundance through the grace and sacrifice of His Son. But, when we turn our thoughts and direct our energies away from God's commandments, we inevitably forfeit the spiritual abundance that might otherwise be ours.

God intends that the institution of marriage should be a continuing source of abundance for husbands and wives alike. But it's up to husbands and wives to claim God's abundance . . . or not.

Have you and your wife accepted God's gift of abundance? If so, your marriage should reflect that decision. When you both honor God and obey Him without reservation, you will receive the love and the abundance that He has promised.

Would you like a formula for a successful marriage? Seek first the kingdom of God and encourage your wife to do likewise. Then, prepare yourselves for the joy, the peace, and the spiritual abundance that the Shepherd offers His sheep.

More from God's Word About Abundance

And God is able to make every grace overflow to you, so that in every way, always having everything you need, you may excel in every good work.

2 Corinthians 9:8 HCSB

Until now you have asked for nothing in My name. Ask and you will receive, that your joy may be complete.

John 16:24 HCSB

Come to terms with God and be at peace; in this way good will come to you.

Job 22:21 HCSB

My cup runs over. Surely goodness and mercy shall follow me all the days of my life; and I will dwell in the house of the Lord forever.

Psalm 23:5-6 NKJV

My purpose is to give life in all its fullness.

John 10:10 HCSB

MORE FROM GOD'S WORD ABOUT GOD'S BLESSINGS

You will show me the path of life; in Your presence is fullness of joy; at Your right hand are pleasures forevermore.

Psalm 16:11 NKJV

For surely, O LORD, you bless the righteous; you surround them with your favor as with a shield.

Psalm 5:12 NIV

The Lord is kind and merciful, slow to get angry, full of unfailing love. The Lord is good to everyone. He showers compassion on all his creation.

Psalm 145:8-9 NLT

Blessed is a man who endures trials, because when he passes the test he will receive the crown of life that He has promised to those who love Him.

James 1:12 HCSB

Unfailing love surrounds those who trust the LORD.

Psalm 32:10 NLT

MORE GREAT IDEAS . . .

God loves you and wants you to experience peace and life—abundant and eternal.

Billy Graham

The gift of God is eternal life, spiritual life, abundant life through faith in Jesus Christ, the Living Word of God.

Anne Graham Lotz

God's riches are beyond anything we could ask or even dare to imagine! If my life gets gooey and stale, I have no excuse.

Barbara Johnson

Yes, we were created for His holy pleasure, but we will ultimately—if not immediately—find much pleasure in His pleasure.

Beth Moore

The only way you can experience abundant life is to surrender your plans to Him.

Charles Stanley

Jesus wants Life for us, Life with a capital L.

John Eldredge

God is the giver, and we are the receivers. And His richest gifts are bestowed not upon those who do the greatest things, but upon those who accept His abundance and His grace.

Hannah Whitall Smith

The Bible says that being a Christian is not only a great way to die, but it's also the best way to live.

Bill Hybels

A TIP FOR HUSBANDS

Do you thank God each day for your wife? And, just as importantly, does your wife know that you're thanking God for her? If so, congratulations. If not, it's time for you to become a lot more thankful and a lot more vocal.

Your Own Ideas About . . .
God's Abundance.

_____

_____

_____

_____

_____

_____

_____

_____

_____

_____

_____

_____

_____

_____

_____

_____

_____

_____

14

"THANK YOU FOR YOUR PATIENCE. I WILL BE PATIENT WITH YOU, TOO."

Love is patient; love is kind.
1 Corinthians 13:4 HCSB

Marriage is an exercise in patience. From time to time, even if your wife is the most considerate woman in the world, she may do things that confound you, confuse you, or anger you. Why? Because even the most considerate woman in the world is still an imperfect human being, capable of missteps, misdeeds, and mistakes. So, because your bride is a fallible yet lovable woman, you should learn to be patient with her shortcomings (just as she, too, must be patient with yours).

Are you one of those guys who demands perfection from everybody, with the possible exception of yourself? If so, it's time to reassess your expectations. God doesn't expect perfection, and neither should you.

Proverbs 19:11 makes it clear: "People with good sense restrain their anger; they earn esteem by overlooking wrongs" (NLT). So the next time you find yourself drumming your fingers while waiting for your wife to do the right thing, take a deep breath and ask God for patience. After all, the world unfolds according to God's timetable, not yours. And your loved ones live—and grow—according to their own timetables, too. Sometimes, you must wait patiently, and that's as it should be. After all, think how patient God has been with you.

MORE FROM GOD'S WORD ABOUT PATIENCE

A patient spirit is better than a proud spirit.

Ecclesiastes 7:8 HCSB

Therefore the Lord is waiting to show you mercy, and is rising up to show you compassion, for the Lord is a just God. Happy are all who wait patiently for Him.

Isaiah 30:18 HCSB

A patient person [shows] great understanding, but a quick-tempered one promotes foolishness.

Proverbs 14:29 HCSB

Rejoice in hope; be patient in affliction; be persistent in prayer.

Romans 12:12 HCSB

Patience is better than power, and controlling one's temper, than capturing a city.

Proverbs 16:32 HCSB

More from God's Word About Kindness

Just as you want others to do for you, do the same for them.

Luke 6:31 HCSB

Finally, all of you be of one mind, having compassion for one another; love as brothers, be tenderhearted, be courteous.

1 Peter 3:8 NKJV

And may the Lord make you increase and abound in love to one another and to all.

1 Thessalonians 3:12 NKJV

And be kind and compassionate to one another, forgiving one another, just as God also forgave you in Christ.

Ephesians 4:32 HCSB

Pure and undefiled religion before our God and Father is this: to look after orphans and widows in their distress and to keep oneself unstained by the world.

James 1:27 HCSB

MORE GREAT IDEAS . . .

Waiting is the hardest kind of work, but God knows best, and we may joyfully leave all in His hands.

Lottie Moon

Waiting is an essential part of spiritual discipline. It can be the ultimate test of faith.

Anne Graham Lotz

By his wisdom, he orders his delays so that they prove to be far better than our hurries.

C. H. Spurgeon

The next time you're disappointed, don't panic. Don't give up. Just be patient and let God remind you he's still in control.

Max Lucado

God never hurries. There are no deadlines against which He must work. To know this is to quiet our spirits and relax our nerves.

A. W. Tozer

He makes us wait. He keeps us in the dark on purpose. He makes us walk when we want to run, sit still when we want to walk, for he has things to do in our souls that we are not interested in.

Elisabeth Elliot

God gave everyone patience—wise people use it.

Anonymous

As we wait on God, He helps us use the winds of adversity to soar above our problems. As the Bible says, "Those who wait on the LORD . . . shall mount up with wings like eagles."

Billy Graham

A TIP FOR HUSBANDS

Do you expect your wife to be patient with you? Then your spouse has the right to expect the same from you. No exceptions.

YOUR OWN IDEAS ABOUT . . .
The Rewards of Being Patient.

_____

_____

_____

_____

_____

_____

_____

_____

_____

_____

_____

_____

_____

_____

_____

_____

_____

_____

15

What Every Husband Should Say to His Wife:

"I CELEBRATE YOUR LOVE, AND I CELEBRATE OUR MARRIAGE."

This is the day the LORD has made;
we will rejoice and be glad in it.
Psalm 118:24 NKJV

How quick are you to celebrate your life, your marriage, and your wife? Christ made it clear to His followers: He intended that His joy would become their joy. And it still holds true today: Christ intends that His believers share His love with joy in their hearts. Yet sometimes, amid the inevitable hustle and bustle of life here on earth, we can forfeit—albeit temporarily—the joy of Christ as we wrestle with the challenges of daily living.

Joy is an important part of healthy Christian marriages. Joyful spouses tend to share their joy with each other, and that's exactly what God intends.

C. H. Spurgeon, the renowned 19th-century English clergyman, advised, "The Lord is glad to open the gate to every knocking soul. It opens very freely; its hinges are not rusted; no bolts secure it. Have faith and enter at this moment through holy courage. If you knock with a heavy heart, you shall yet sing with joy of spirit. Never be discouraged!"

Are you doing your best to live each day as a joyful servant of Christ? And, are you inviting your wife to join in the celebration? Hopefully so. After all, few things in life are more wonderful to behold than the joining together of two joyful believers. So now, with no further ado, thank God for your marriage, and let the celebration begin!

MORE FROM GOD'S WORD ABOUT CELEBRATING LIFE

David and the whole house of Israel were celebrating before the Lord.

2 Samuel 6:5 HCSB

Their sorrow was turned into rejoicing and their mourning into a holiday. They were to be days of feasting, rejoicing, and of sending gifts to one another and the poor.

Esther 9:22 HCSB

At the dedication of the wall of Jerusalem, they sent for the Levites wherever they lived and brought them to Jerusalem to celebrate the joyous dedication with thanksgiving and singing accompanied by cymbals, harps, and lyres.

Nehemiah 12:27 HCSB

Then he said to them, "Go and eat what is rich, drink what is sweet, and send portions to those who have nothing prepared, since today is holy to our Lord. Do not grieve, because your strength [comes from] rejoicing in the Lord."

Nehemiah 8:10 HCSB

MORE FROM GOD'S WORD ABOUT BEING JOYFUL

Rejoice in the Lord always. I will say it again: Rejoice!

Philippians 4:4 HCSB

Delight yourself also in the Lord, and He shall give you the desires of your heart.

Psalm 37:4 NKJV

Make me hear joy and gladness.

Psalm 51:8 NKJV

Weeping may spend the night, but there is joy in the morning.

Psalms 30:5 HCSB

The Lord reigns; let the earth rejoice.

Psalm 97:1 NKJV

More Great Ideas . . .

Joy is the direct result of having God's perspective on our daily lives and the effect of loving our Lord enough to obey His commands and trust His promises.

Bill Bright

Our sense of joy, satisfaction, and fulfillment in life increases, no matter what the circumstances, if we are in the center of God's will.

Billy Graham

He wants us to have a faith that does not complain while waiting, but rejoices because we know our times are in His hands—nail-scarred hands that labor for our highest good.

Kay Arthur

Lord, I thank you for the promise of heaven and the unexpected moments when you touch my heartstrings with that longing for my eternal home.

Joni Eareckson Tada

My meditation and study have shown me that, like God, His Word is holy, everlasting, absolutely true, powerful, personally fair, and never changing.

Bill Bright

Words fail to express my love for this holy Book, my gratitude for its author, for His love and goodness. How shall I thank him for it?

Lottie Moon

Meditating upon His Word will inevitably bring peace of mind, strength of purpose, and power for living.

Bill Bright

A TIP FOR HUSBANDS

God has given you and your wife the gift of life (here on earth) and the promise of eternal life (in heaven). Now, He wants you to celebrate those gifts. The rest, of course, is up to you.

YOUR OWN IDEAS ABOUT . . .
The Rewards of Celebrating Your Marriage
and Your Faith.

_____

_____

_____

_____

_____

_____

_____

_____

_____

_____

_____

_____

_____

_____

_____

_____

16

What Every Husband Should Say to His Wife:

"THANK YOU FOR BEING FAITHFUL WHEN TIMES ARE TOUGH."

Mighty waters cannot extinguish love;
rivers cannot sweep it away.
Song of Solomon 8:7 HCSB

L ife is a tapestry of good days and difficult days, with the good days predominating. When times are good, we are tempted to take our blessings for granted. But, when times are tough, we discover precisely what we're made of.

Every marriage, like every life, will encounter days of hardship and pain. It is only then that husbands and wives can discover precisely what their marriage is made of.

When we experience a deeply significant loss, we must learn (once again) to trust God and to trust those who love us most. When we do, we come to understand that our suffering carries with it great potential: the potential for intense personal growth and the potential to add depth and meaning to our relationships.

Are you and your wife enduring tough times? If so, hold tightly to each other and turn your hearts toward God. When you do, you may rest assured that the two of you—plus God—can handle anything that comes your way.

MORE FROM GOD'S WORD ABOUT ADVERSITY

We are pressured in every way but not crushed; we are perplexed but not in despair.

2 Corinthians 4:8 HCSB

He heals the brokenhearted, and binds their wounds.

Psalm 147:3 NASB

I called to the Lord in my distress; I called to my God. From His temple He heard my voice.

2 Samuel 22:7 HCSB

A righteous man may have many troubles, but the LORD delivers him from them all . . . .

Psalm 34:19 NIV

Consider it a great joy, my brothers, whenever you experience various trials, knowing that the testing of your faith produces endurance. But endurance must do its complete work, so that you may be mature and complete, lacking nothing.

James 1:2-4 HCSB

MORE FROM GOD'S WORD ABOUT ANXIETY

When you pass through the waters, I will be with you; and through the rivers, they shall not overflow you. When you walk through the fire, you shall not be burned, nor shall the flame scorch you. For I am the Lord your God, The Holy One of Israel, your Savior.

Isaiah 43:2-3 NKJV

Cast all your anxiety on him because he cares for you.

1 Peter 5:7 NIV

Be anxious for nothing, but in everything by prayer and supplication with thanksgiving let your requests be made known to God.

Philippians 4:6 NASB

Let not your heart be troubled: ye believe in God, believe also in me.

John 14:1 KJV

So don't worry about tomorrow, because tomorrow will have its own worries. Each day has enough trouble of its own.

Matthew 6:34 NCV

MORE GREAT IDEAS . . .

Of course marriage can be difficult! For sure, there will be times you are inwardly convinced you can't go on. But I remind you of your vow, your stated commitment: "...for better, for worse...." What you are experiencing may be some of the "worse." And no marriage is exempt from such times.

Charles Swindoll

Those who abandon ship the first time it enters a storm miss the calm beyond. And the rougher the storms weathered together, the deeper and stronger real love grows.

Ruth Bell Graham

Real love has staying power. Authentic love is tough love. It refuses to look for ways to run away. It always opts for working through.

Charles Swindoll

As a child of God, rest in the knowledge that your Savior precedes you, and He will walk with you through each experience of your life.

Henry Blackaby

Father and Mother lived on the edge of poverty, and yet their contentment was not dependent upon their surroundings. Their relationship to each other and to the Lord gave them strength and happiness.

Corrie ten Boom

We should not be upset when unexpected and upsetting things happen. God, in His wisdom, means to make something of us which we have not yet attained, and He is dealing with us accordingly.

J. I. Packer

A Tip for Husbands

If you're having tough times, don't hit the panic button and don't keep everything bottled up inside. Talk things over with your wife, and if necessary, find a counselor you can really trust. A second opinion (or, for that matter, a third, fourth, or fifth opinion) is usually helpful. So if your troubles seem overwhelming, be willing to seek outside help—starting, of course, with your pastor.

YOUR OWN IDEAS ABOUT . . .
How You and Your Wife Deal with Adversity.

_____

_____

_____

_____

_____

_____

_____

_____

_____

_____

_____

_____

_____

_____

_____

_____

_____

17

What Every Husband Should Say to His Wife:

"TIME HERE ON EARTH IS SHORT AND PRECIOUS. I WANT TO SPEND AS MUCH OF IT WITH YOU AS I CAN."

*To everything there is a season,
a time for every purpose under heaven.*

Ecclesiastes 3:1 NKJV

If you sincerely want your marriage to flourish, then you should be prepared to invest the time and energy required to do so. Wise couples invest time—high quality time—nurturing their relationships. And it shows.

Time is a precious, nonrenewable gift from God. But sometimes, we treat our time here on earth as if it were not a gift at all: We may be tempted to waste time in countless ways, and when we do so, we pay a high price for our mistaken priorities.

How are you choosing to spend the time that God has given you? Are you carving out large blocks of time to spend with your wife? Or are you wasting precious days rushing after the countless distractions and temptations that the world has to offer?

As you establish priorities for your day and your life, remember that each new day is a special treasure to be savored and celebrated with your loved ones. As a Christian couple, you and your wife have much to celebrate and much to do. It's up to both of you to honor God for the gift of time by using that gift wisely . . . and using it together.

MORE FROM GOD'S WORD ABOUT YOUR TIME

Therefore humble yourselves under the mighty hand of God, that He may exalt you in due time.

1 Peter 5:6 NKJV

I wait for the Lord, my soul waits, and in His word I do hope. My soul waits for the Lord more than those who watch for the morning—yes, more than those who watch for the morning.

Psalm 130:5-6 NKJV

He has made everything appropriate in its time. He has also put eternity in their hearts, but man cannot discover the work God has done from beginning to end.

Ecclesiastes 3:11 HCSB

Therefore the Lord is waiting to show you mercy, and is rising up to show you compassion, for the Lord is a just God. Happy are all who wait patiently for Him.

Isaiah 30:18 HCSB

MORE GREAT IDEAS . . .

It's sobering to contemplate how much time, effort, sacrifice, compromise, and attention we give to acquiring and increasing our supply of something that is totally insignificant in eternity.

Anne Graham Lotz

Great relief and satisfaction can come from seeking God's priorities for us in each season, discerning what is "best" in the midst of many noble opportunities, and pouring our most excellent energies into those things.

Beth Moore

Sin is largely a matter of mistaken priorities. Any sin in us that is cherished, hidden, and not confessed will cut the nerve center of our faith.

Catherine Marshall

If choosing to spend time alone with God is a real struggle—a heavy-handed demand that only adds more guilt and stress to your already overblown schedule—it's time to change the way you approach his presence.

Doris Greig

Don't stop the plough to kill a mouse. Do not hinder important business for the discussion of a trifle.

C. H. Spurgeon

One hundred years from now it won't matter if you got that big break, or finally traded up to a Mercedes. It will greatly matter, one hundred years from now, that you made a commitment to Jesus Christ.

David Shibley

The essence of the Christian life is Jesus: that in all things He might have the preeminence, not that in some things He might have a place.

Franklin Graham

A Tip for Husbands

The real currency of family life is time, not dollars. Wise husbands give generous amounts of time to their wives.

YOUR OWN IDEAS ABOUT . . .
Ways That You and Your Wife Can Spend
More Time Together.

_____

_____

_____

_____

_____

_____

_____

_____

_____

_____

_____

_____

_____

_____

_____

_____

18

What Every Husband Should Say to His Wife:

"THANK YOU FOR YOUR INTEGRITY. IT ENRICHES OUR MARRIAGE."

A wife of noble character who can find?
She is worth far more than rubies.
Proverbs 31:10 NIV

Proverbs 31:10 reminds thoughtful husbands (like you) that a wife of noble character is a blessing from God, a priceless gift from above, a treasure that should be valued and protected.

Of course you already know how deeply you value your bride, but do you communicate your gratitude with words every day? And do you demonstrate your gratitude with courtesy and kindness seven days a week? If you sincerely want to be a wise husband, and a good one, that's precisely what you'll do.

A woman of strong character should be esteemed, especially in today's troubled society. After all, she inhabits a world where temptations and distractions are everywhere, or so it seems. Yet noble women, women like your wife, remain loyal and steadfast.

So today and every day, give your thanks and admiration to that good woman with whom you share your life and your marriage. She is, indeed, priceless. She is worthy of your praise.

More from God's Word About Character

A woman who fears the Lord will be praised.

Proverbs 31:30 HCSB

A good name is to be chosen rather than great riches, loving favor rather than silver and gold.

Proverbs 22:1 NKJV

Do not be deceived: "Evil company corrupts good habits."

1 Corinthians 15:33 NKJV

In all things showing yourself to be a pattern of good works; in doctrine showing integrity, reverence, incorruptibility . . . .

Titus 2:7 NKJV

Let integrity and uprightness preserve me, for I wait for You.

Psalm 25:21 NKJV

MORE FROM GOD'S WORD ABOUT HONESTY

These are the things you must do: Speak truth to one another; render honest and peaceful judgments in your gates.

Zechariah 8:16 HCSB

The one who lives with integrity lives securely, but whoever perverts his ways will be found out.

Proverbs 10:9 HCSB

The one who lives with integrity will be helped, but one who distorts right and wrong will suddenly fall.

Proverbs 28:18 HCSB

In everything set them an example by doing what is good. In your teaching show integrity, seriousness and soundness of speech that cannot be condemned, so that those who oppose you may be ashamed because they have nothing bad to say about us.

Titus 2:7 NIV

125

More Great Ideas . . .

The trials of life can be God's tools for engraving His image on our character.

Warren Wiersbe

There is no way to grow a saint overnight. Character, like the oak tree, does not spring up like a mushroom.

Vance Havner

In matters of style, swim with the current. In matters of principle, stand like a rock.

Thomas Jefferson

Character is both developed and revealed by tests, and all of life is a test.

Rick Warren

Maintaining your integrity in a world of sham is no small accomplishment.

Wayne Oates

Character is made in the small moments of our lives.

Phillips Brooks

Each one of us is God's special work of art. Through us, He teaches and inspires, delights and encourages, informs and uplifts all those who view our lives. God, the master artist, is most concerned about expressing Himself—His thoughts and His intentions—through what He paints in our characters.

Joni Eareckson Tada

Image is what people think we are; integrity is what we really are.

John Maxwell

A Tip for Husbands

Never be afraid of praising your wife too much, but be very afraid of praising her too little.

YOUR OWN IDEAS ABOUT . . .
The Rewards of Being Married to an Honorable Woman.

_____

_____

_____

_____

_____

_____

_____

_____

_____

_____

_____

_____

_____

_____

_____

_____

_____

_____

19

"YOU ALWAYS
BRING ME JOY."

*Be happy with the wife you married when you were young.
She gives you joy, as your fountain gives you water.*
Proverbs 5:18 NCV

Does your wife know that she brings you great joy? Do you tell her so? And do you show her, by your words and your actions, that you are a joyful man, who appreciates God's blessings? Hopefully so. After all, you and your wife have many reasons to be grateful: God is in His heaven; Christ has risen, and you are the sheep of His flock. And, God has brought the two of you together, not just for a lifetime, but for eternity. So what's not to celebrate? Yet sometimes, even the most devout couples may become discouraged. After all, we live in a world where expectations can be high and demands can be even higher.

When we fail to meet the expectations of others (or, for that matter, the expectations that we have for ourselves), we may be tempted to abandon hope. But God has other plans. He knows exactly how He intends to use us. Our task is to remain faithful until He does.

If you or your wife become discouraged by the direction of life, turn your thoughts and prayers to God. He is a God of possibility, not negativity. He will help you count your blessings instead of your hardships. Then, with a renewed spirit of optimism and hope, you can properly thank your Father in heaven for His blessings, for His love, and for His Son.

MORE FROM GOD'S WORD ABOUT JOY

These things I have spoken to you, that My joy may remain in you, and that your joy may be full.

John 15:11 NKJV

A joyful heart is good medicine, but a broken spirit dries up the bones.

Proverbs 17:22 NASB

Always be full of joy in the Lord. I say it again—rejoice!

Philippians 4:4 NLT

Rejoice, and be exceeding glad: for great is your reward in heaven....

Matthew 5:12 KJV

Shout for joy to the LORD, all the earth. Worship the LORD with gladness; come before him with joyful songs.

Psalm 100:1-2 NIV

MORE GREAT IDEAS . . .

Attitude is more important than the past, than education, than money, than circumstances, than what people do or say. It is more important than appearance, giftedness, or skill.

Charles Swindoll

The mind is like a clock that is constantly running down. It has to be wound up daily with good thoughts.

Fulton J. Sheen

The difference between winning and losing is how we choose to react to disappointment.

Barbara Johnson

I have witnessed many attitudes make a positive turn-around through prayer.

John Maxwell

It's your choice: you can either count your blessings or recount your disappointments.

Jim Gallery

The Reference Point for the Christian is the Bible. All values, judgments, and attitudes must be gauged in relationship to this Reference Point.

Ruth Bell Graham

Attitude is the mind's paintbrush; it can color any situation.

Barbara Johnson

Life is 10% what happens to you and 90% how you respond to it.

Charles Swindoll

A TIP FOR HUSBANDS

Every day, God gives you many reasons to rejoice. The rest is up to you.

Your Own Ideas About . . .
The Joys of Being a Husband and a Father.

_____

_____

_____

_____

_____

_____

_____

_____

_____

_____

_____

_____

_____

_____

_____

_____

_____

20

What Every Husband Should Say to His Wife:

"YOU BRING SUCH JOY AND HAPPINESS TO OUR MARRIAGE. I AM SO GRATEFUL THAT GOD BROUGHT US TOGETHER."

Live happily with the woman you love . . . .
The wife God gives you is your reward for all
your earthly toil.

Ecclesiastes 9:9 NLT

God wants you and your wife to experience a happy marriage. And, of course, your intentions are the same. But how, exactly, can you experience the full measure of joy that God intends for you and your bride to share? A great place to start is by allowing yourself to become genuinely enthusiastic about your marriage and your life.

Are you excited about your marriage? Do you feel good about yourself, your wife, your kids, your friends, and your situation? And do you see each day as a glorious opportunity to serve God and to do His will? Hopefully so. After all, you were created in God's image, and He has blessed you in more ways than you can count. Now, it's your job to thank Him with words of praise and a life that is praiseworthy.

Psalm 100 reminds us that, as believers, we have every reason to celebrate: "Shout for joy to the LORD, all the earth. Worship the LORD with gladness" (vv. 1-2 NIV). Yet sometimes, amid the inevitable hustle and bustle of life here on earth, we can forfeit—albeit temporarily—the joy that God intends for our lives.

Few things in life are more sad, or, for that matter, more absurd, than the sight of a grumpy Christian couple bickering their way through life. After all, Christ offers all His believers the possibility of joy and abundance—but He does not force His joy upon us. We must claim that joy for ourselves, as must our loved ones. When we do, Jesus, in turn, fills our spirits with His power and His love. Then, we can share Christ's joy and His message with a world that needs both.

MORE FROM GOD'S WORD ABOUT HAPPINESS

Rejoice always, pray without ceasing, in everything give thanks; for this is the will of God in Christ Jesus for you.

1 Thessalonians 5:16-18 NKJV

But the man who looks intently into the perfect law that gives freedom, and continues to do this, not forgetting what he has heard, but doing it—he will be blessed in what he does.

James 1:25 NIV

How happy are those who can live in your house, always singing your praises. How happy are those who are strong in the Lord . . . .

Psalm 84:4-5 NLT

MORE FROM GOD'S WORD ABOUT CONTENTMENT

I have learned to be content in whatever circumstances I am.

Philippians 4:11 HCSB

A tranquil heart is life to the body, but jealousy is rottenness to the bones.

Proverbs 14:30 HCSB

The LORD will give strength to His people; the LORD will bless His people with peace.

Psalm 29:11 NKJV

Let your conduct be without covetousness; be content with such things as you have. For He Himself has said, "I will never leave you nor forsake you."

Hebrews 13:5 NKJV

But godliness with contentment is a great gain.

1 Timothy 6:6 HCSB

MORE GREAT IDEAS . . .

People who have invested their lives in worthwhile pursuits have discovered a measure of happiness.

Warren Wiersbe

I became aware of one very important concept I had missed before: my attitude—not my circumstances—was what was making me unhappy.

Vonette Bright

We will never be happy until we make God the source of our fulfillment and the answer to our longings.

Stormie Omartian

The secret of a happy life is to delight in duty. When duty becomes delight, then burdens become blessings.

Warren Wiersbe

This is the happy life: to rejoice to Thee, of Thee, for Thee; this it is, and there is no other.

St. Augustine

I am truly happy with Jesus Christ. I couldn't live without Him.

Ruth Bell Graham

Christ is the secret, the source, the substance, the center, and the circumference of all true and lasting gladness.

Mrs. Charles E. Cowman

God's goal is not to make you happy. It is to make you his.

Max Lucado

A TIP FOR HUSBANDS

Happy marriages are not perfect marriages. They are marriages between two imperfect people who choose to be happy despite each other's imperfections.

YOUR OWN IDEAS ABOUT . . .

Simple Ways You Can Make Your Wife a Little Happier.

_____

_____

_____

_____

_____

_____

_____

_____

_____

_____

_____

_____

_____

_____

_____

_____

_____

21

What Every Husband Should Say to His Wife:

"You Are Beautiful in Every Way."

Your beauty should not come from outward adornment,
such as braided hair and the wearing of gold jewelry
and fine clothes. Instead, it should be that of your inner self,
the unfading beauty of a gentle and quiet spirit,
which is of great worth in God's sight.

1 Peter 3:3-4 NIV

Society's brand of feminine beauty is decidedly non-spiritual because it's based solely on appearances. But God sees the heart. He sees the real woman of the woman you love, and so should you.

As your wife's biggest booster, you must have a clear understanding of the real attributes that make your bride beautiful, and you must strive to convince her that her beauty is apparent to you and to the world. But sometimes, convincing her of her beauty won't be easy.

The media is working around the clock in an attempt to make your wife feel inferior, to convince her that she won't measure up until she changes something about herself, until she becomes thinner, or younger looking, or until she spends untold amounts of time and money changing her outward appearance. Your job, as a loving husband, is to remind your wife that she need not make any changes to be beautiful.

Genuine beauty begins on the inside and works its way out from there. So if you're wise, you'll take time each day to praise your bride for her outer beauty (which the world sees) but even more time to praise her for her inner beauty (which God sees). And while you're at it, you'll remind her that she doesn't ever have to be perfect to be perfectly lovely.

MORE FROM GOD'S WORD ABOUT BEAUTY

He has made everything beautiful in its time.

Ecclesiastes 3:11 NIV

If you decide for God, living a life of God-worship, it follows that you don't fuss about what's on the table at mealtimes or whether the clothes in your closet are in fashion. There is far more to your life than the food you put in your stomach, more to your outer appearance than the clothes you hang on your body.

Matthew 6:25 MSG

And let the beauty of the Lord our God be upon us.

Psalm 90:17 NKJV

Man does not see what the Lord sees, for man sees what is visible, but the Lord sees the heart.

1 Samuel 16:7 HCSB

MORE GREAT IDEAS . . .

I truly believe that the longing to be known as beautiful is a part of our design as women. God put us together this way on purpose. We are wired to long for beauty and to be known as beautiful, yet the world does a wonderful job of squelching this desire.

Angela Thomas

No matter how old they grow, some people never lose their beauty. They merely move it from their faces into their hearts.

Barbara Johnson

Some of the most ordinary looking women imaginable by the world's standards possess a beauty that is utterly striking because of the condition of their hearts.

Ed Young

God's fingers can touch nothing but to mould it into loveliness.

George MacDonald

Knowing God's sovereignty and unconditional love imparts a beauty to life . . . and to you.

Kay Arthur

God who is goodness and truth is also beauty. It is this innate human and divine longing, found in the company of goodness and truth, that is able to recognize and leap up at beauty and rejoice and know that all is beautiful, that there is not one speck of beauty under the sun that does not mirror back the beauty of God.

Roberta Bondi

The splendor of a soul in grace is so seductive that it surpasses the beauty of all created things.

Thomas Aquinas

A Tip for Husbands

If you truly believe that beauty begins on the inside, make sure your words and actions match your beliefs. Your wife doesn't deserve to hear mixed messages.

YOUR OWN IDEAS ABOUT . . .
Simple Ways You Can Remind Your Wife
That She Is Beautiful.

_____

_____

_____

_____

_____

_____

_____

_____

_____

_____

_____

_____

_____

_____

_____

_____

22

What Every Husband Should Say to His Wife:

"I PRAISE GOD FOR YOU AND FOR OUR MARRIAGE."

It is good to give thanks to the Lord, to sing praises to the Most High. It is good to proclaim your unfailing love in the morning, your faithfulness in the evening.

Psalm 92:1-2 NLT

It's easy to "compartmentalize" our waking hours into a few familiar categories: work, rest, play, family time, and worship. As creatures of habit, we may find ourselves praising God only at particular times of the day or on a particular day of the week. But praise for our Creator should never be reserved for mealtimes, bedtimes, or church. Instead, we should praise God all day, every day, to the greatest extent we can, with thanksgiving in our hearts, and with a song on our lips.

Worship and praise should be woven into the fabric of everything we do; they should not be relegated to a weekly three-hour visit to church on Sunday morning. A. W. Tozer correctly observed, "If you will not worship God seven days a week, you do not worship Him on one day a week."

Do you praise God many times each day? And do you thank Him specifically for your wife and family? If so, keep up the good work; if not, it's time to reassess your priorities. When you consider the wonderful things that God has done for you, you'll find the time—or more accurately you'll make the time—to praise Him for all that He has done.

Every time you notice a gift from the Creator, thank Him and praise Him. His works are marvelous, His gifts are beyond understanding, and His love endures forever.

More from God's Word About Praising Him

Praise him, all you people of the earth, for he loves us with unfailing love; the faithfulness of the Lord endures forever. Praise the Lord!

Psalm 117 NLT

I will praise the Lord at all times, I will constantly speak his praises.

Psalm 34:1 NLT

Through Him then, let us continually offer up a sacrifice of praise to God, that is, the fruit of lips that give thanks to His name.

Hebrews 13:15 NASB

Because of this, God raised him up to the heights of heaven and gave him a name that is above every other name, so that at the name of Jesus every knee will bow, in heaven and on earth and under the earth, and every tongue will confess that Jesus Christ is Lord, to the glory of God the Father.

Philippians 2:9-11 NLT

MORE FROM GOD'S WORD ABOUT HIS WISDOM

The fear of the Lord is the beginning of wisdom; a good understanding have all those who do His commandments. His praise endures forever.

Psalm 111:10 NKJV

So teach us to number our days, that we may gain a heart of wisdom.

Psalm 90:12 NKJV

Teach me, O Lord, the way of Your statutes, and I shall keep it to the end.

Psalm 119:33 NKJV

A wise man will hear and increase learning, and a man of understanding will attain wise counsel.

Proverbs 1:5 NKJV

Acquire wisdom—how much better it is than gold! And acquire understanding—it is preferable to silver.

Proverbs 16:16 HCSB

MORE GREAT IDEAS . . .

Words fail to express my love for this holy Book, my gratitude for its author, for His love and goodness. How shall I thank him for it?

Lottie Moon

A child of God should be a visible beatitude for joy and a living doxology for gratitude.

C. H. Spurgeon

The time for universal praise is sure to come some day. Let us begin to do our part now.

Hannah Whitall Smith

Praise reestablishes the proper chain of command; we recognize that the King is on the throne and that he has saved his people.

Max Lucado

Nothing we do is more powerful or more life-changing than praising God.

Stormie Omartian

Our God is the sovereign Creator of the universe! He loves us as His own children and has provided every good thing we have; He is worthy of our praise every moment.

Shirley Dobson

Holy, holy, holy! Lord God Almighty! All Thy works shall praise Thy name in earth, and sky, and sea.

Reginald Heber

Praise is the highest occupation of any being.

Max Lucado

A TIP FOR HUSBANDS

Remember that it always pays to praise your Creator. That's why thoughtful believers (like you) make it a habit to carve out quiet moments throughout the day to praise God.

YOUR OWN IDEAS ABOUT . . .
The Rewards of Praising God.

_____

_____

_____

_____

_____

_____

_____

_____

_____

_____

_____

_____

_____

_____

_____

_____

_____

_____

23

"I WILL NEVER STOP LOVING YOU."

*So we must not get tired of doing good,
for we will reap at the proper time if we don't give up.*

Galatians 6:9 HCSB

Your wife needs to know that you love her today, that you will love her tomorrow, and that you will love her forever. Marriage is, after all, a marathon, not a sprint—and couples who expect otherwise will be sadly disappointed. That's why husbands and wives need large quantities of patience, forgiveness, hope, and perseverance.

Every marriage and every life has its share of roadblocks and stumbling blocks; these situations require courage and determination. As an example of perfect courage and steadfast determination, we need look no further than our Savior, Jesus Christ.

Jesus finished what He began. Despite the torture He endured, despite the shame of the cross, Jesus was steadfast in His faithfulness to God. We, too, must remain faithful— faithful to God, faithful to our principles, and faithful to our loved ones—especially during times of transition or hardship.

The next time you are tempted to give up on yourself, your duties, or your relationships, ask yourself this question: "What would Jesus have me do?" When you find the answer to that question, you'll know precisely what to do.

MORE FROM GOD'S WORD ABOUT PERSEVERANCE

Do you not know that the runners in a stadium all race, but only one receives the prize? Run in such a way that you may win. Now everyone who competes exercises self-control in everything. However, they do it to receive a perishable crown, but we an imperishable one.

1 Corinthians 9:24-25 HCSB

But as for you, be strong; don't be discouraged, for your work has a reward.

2 Chronicles 15:7 HCSB

Let us lay aside every weight and the sin that so easily ensnares us, and run with endurance the race that lies before us, keeping our eyes on Jesus, the source and perfecter of our faith.

Hebrews 12:1-2 HCSB

Now we want each of you to demonstrate the same diligence for the final realization of your hope, so that you won't become lazy, but imitators of those who inherit the promises through faith and perseverance.

Hebrews 6:11-12 HCSB

MORE FROM GOD'S WORD ABOUT RENEWAL

But may the God of all grace, who called us to His eternal glory by Christ Jesus, after you have suffered a while, perfect, establish, strengthen, and settle you.

1 Peter 5:10 NKJV

Finally, brothers, rejoice. Be restored, be encouraged, be of the same mind, be at peace, and the God of love and peace will be with you.

2 Corinthians 13:11 HCSB

But those who wait on the Lord shall renew their strength; they shall mount up with wings like eagles, they shall run and not be weary, they shall walk and not faint.

Isaiah 40:31 NKJV

Therefore if anyone is in Christ, he is a new creature; the old things passed away; behold, new things have come.

2 Corinthians 5:17 HCSB

You are being renewed in the spirit of your minds; you put on the new man, the one created according to God's likeness in righteousness and purity of the truth.

Ephesians 4:23-24 HCSB

MORE GREAT IDEAS . . .

In the Bible, patience is not a passive acceptance of circumstances. It is a courageous perseverance in the face of suffering and difficulty.

Warren Wiersbe

Achievers refused to hold on to the common excuses for failure. They turned their stumbling blocks into stepping stones. They realized that they couldn't determine every circumstance in life but they could determine their choice of attitude towards every circumstance.

John Maxwell

Battles are won in the trenches, in the grit and grime of courageous determination; they are won day by day in the arena of life.

Charles Swindoll

Failure is one of life's most powerful teachers. How we handle our failures determines whether we're going to simply "get by" in life or "press on."

Beth Moore

In all negotiations of difficulties, a man may not look to sow and reap at once. He must prepare his business and so ripen it by degrees.

Francis Bacon

Jesus taught that perseverance is the essential element in prayer.

E. M. Bounds

Every achievement worth remembering is stained with the blood of diligence and scarred by the wounds of disappointment.

Charles Swindoll

A Tip for Husbands

Remember the words of Winston Churchill: He's the wise man who said, "Never give in; never give in; never give in." If Churchill hadn't been the Prime Minister of England, he would have made a pretty good marriage counselor.

YOUR OWN IDEAS ABOUT . . .
The Power of Perseverance.

_____

_____

_____

_____

_____

_____

_____

_____

_____

_____

_____

_____

_____

_____

_____

_____

_____

_____

_____

24

"I UNDERSTAND THAT
WE ARE ON
A SPIRITUAL JOURNEY."

*But grow in the grace and knowledge of our Lord
and Savior Jesus Christ. To Him be the glory both now
and to the day of eternity.*

2 Peter 3:18 HCSB

At its best, a Christian marriage is: a partnership between two believers who embark upon a lifelong journey toward spiritual maturity and growth. No Christian couple should ever be completely satisfied with the condition of their spiritual health; instead, they should continue to grow in the love and the knowledge of their Savior.

When we cease to grow, either emotionally or spiritually, we do ourselves and our loved ones a profound disservice. But, if we study God's Word, if we obey His commandments, and if we live in the center of His will, we will not be stagnant believers; we will, instead, be growing Christians . . . and that's exactly what God wants for our marriages and our lives.

Does your wife encourage your spiritual growth, and is the reverse also true? If so, you are to be congratulated. If not, it's time for change. After all, God doesn't want you (or your marriage) to be stagnant. He wants you to keep growing and growing. And that's exactly what you should want, too.

MORE FROM GOD'S WORD ABOUT
SPIRITUAL GROWTH

For this reason also, since the day we heard this, we haven't stopped praying for you. We are asking that you may be filled with the knowledge of His will in all wisdom and spiritual understanding.

Colossians 1:9 HCSB

For though by this time you ought to be teachers, you need someone to teach you again the basic principles of God's revelation. You need milk, not solid food. Now everyone who lives on milk is inexperienced with the message about righteousness, because he is an infant. But solid food is for the mature—for those whose senses have been trained to distinguish between good and evil.

Hebrews 5:12-14 HCSB

But the natural man does not welcome what comes from God's Spirit, because it is foolishness to him; he is not able to know it since it is evaluated spiritually. The spiritual person, however, can evaluate everything, yet he himself cannot be evaluated by anyone.

1 Corinthians 2:14-15 HCSB

MORE FROM GOD'S WORD ABOUT LISTENING TO YOUR CONSCIENCE

So I strive always to keep my conscience clear before God and man.

Acts 24:16 NIV

Let us draw near to God with a sincere heart in full assurance of faith, having our hearts sprinkled to cleanse us from a guilty conscience and having our bodies washed with pure water.

Hebrews 10:22 NIV

I will maintain my righteousness and never let go of it; my conscience will not reproach me as long as I live.

Job 27:6 NIV

Do not conform any longer to the pattern of this world, but be transformed by the renewing of your mind. Then you will be able to test and approve what God's will is—his good, pleasing and perfect will.

Romans 12:2 NIV

Create in me a pure heart, O God, and renew a steadfast spirit within me.

Psalm 51:10 NIV

MORE GREAT IDEAS . . .

We've grown to be one soul—two parts; our lives are so intertwined that when some passion stirs your heart, I feel the quake in mine.

Gloria Gaither

Growth takes place in quietness, in hidden ways, in silence and solitude. The process is not accessible to observation.

Eugene Peterson

We often become mentally and spiritually barren because we're so busy.

Franklin Graham

The vigor of our spiritual lives will be in exact proportion to the place held by the Bible in our lives and in our thoughts.

George Mueller

God's plan for our guidance is for us to grow gradually in wisdom before we get to the crossroads.

Bill Hybels

A Christian is never in a state of completion but always in the process of becoming.

Martin Luther

Spiritual growth consists most in the growth of the root, which is out of sight.

Matthew Henry

We look at our burdens and heavy loads, and we shrink from them. But, if we lift them and bind them about our hearts, they become wings, and on them we can rise and soar toward God.

Mrs. Charles E. Cowman

A TIP FOR HUSBANDS

Today, talk to your wife about the strength that can be yours when you allow Christ to dwell at the center of your marriage.

YOUR OWN IDEAS ABOUT . . .
The Rewards That Can Be Yours If You
Keep Growing Spiritually.

_____

_____

_____

_____

_____

_____

_____

_____

_____

_____

_____

_____

_____

_____

_____

_____

25

What Every Husband Should Say to His Wife:

"I KNOW THAT LIFE IS SHORT, SO I TREASURE THE TIME WE SPEND TOGETHER."

Enjoy life with the wife you love all the days of your fleeting life, which has been given to you under the sun, all your fleeting days.

Ecclesiastes 9:9 HCSB

It takes time to build a strong marriage . . . lots of time. Yet we live in a world where time seems to be an ever-shrinking commodity as we rush from place to place with seldom a moment to spare.

Has the busy pace of life robbed you of high-quality time with your bride? If so, it's time to adjust your priorities. And God can help.

When you fervently ask God to help you prioritize your life, He will give you guidance. When you seek His guidance every day, your Creator will reveal Himself in a variety of ways. As a follower of Christ, you must do no less.

When you allow God to help you organize your day, you'll soon discover that there is ample time for your spouse and your family. When you make God a full partner in every aspect of your life, He will lead you along the proper path: His path. When you allow God to reign over your heart, He will honor you with spiritual blessings that are simply too numerous to count. So, as you plan for the day ahead, make God's priorities your priorities. When you do, every other priority will have a tendency to fall neatly into place.

MORE FROM GOD'S WORD ABOUT PRIORITIES

He said to them all, "If anyone desires to come after Me, let him deny himself, and take up his cross daily, and follow Me. For whoever desires to save his life will lose it, but whoever loses his life for My sake will save it."

Luke 9:23-24 NKJV

Don't abandon wisdom, and she will watch over you; love her, and she will guard you.

Proverbs 4:6 HCSB

And I pray this: that your love will keep on growing in knowledge and every kind of discernment, so that you can determine what really matters and can be pure and blameless in the day of Christ.

Philippians 1:9 HCSB

And He said to them, "Take heed and beware of covetousness, for one's life does not consist in the abundance of the things he possesses."

Luke 12:15 NKJV

MORE FROM GOD'S WORD ABOUT TODAY

Working together with Him, we also appeal to you: "Don't receive God's grace in vain." For He says: In an acceptable time, I heard you, and in the day of salvation, I helped you. Look, now is the acceptable time; look, now is the day of salvation.

2 Corinthians 6:1-2 HCSB

I must work the works of Him who sent Me while it is day; the night is coming when no one can work.

John 9:4 NKJV

Therefore, get your minds ready for action, being self-disciplined, and set your hope completely on the grace to be brought to you at the revelation of Jesus Christ.

1 Peter 1:13 HCSB

So teach us to number our days, that we may gain a heart of wisdom.

Psalm 90:12 NKJV

MORE GREAT IDEAS . . .

It is important to know that you have to work to keep love alive; you have to protect it and maintain it, just like you would a delicate flower.

James Dobson

It's sobering to contemplate how much time, effort, sacrifice, compromise, and attention we give to acquiring and increasing our supply of something that is totally insignificant in eternity.

Anne Graham Lotz

The essence of the Christian life is Jesus: that in all things He might have the preeminence, not that in some things He might have a place.

Franklin Graham

Great relief and satisfaction can come from seeking God's priorities for us in each season, discerning what is "best" in the midst of many noble opportunities, and pouring our most excellent energies into those things.

Beth Moore

Sin is largely a matter of mistaken priorities. Any sin in us that is cherished, hidden, and not confessed will cut the nerve center of our faith.

Catherine Marshall

Give me the person who says, "This one thing I do, and not these fifty things I dabble in."

D. L. Moody

A marriage can't survive forever on leftovers. It needs to be fed continually, or it will eventually starve.

John Maxwell

A TIP FOR HUSBANDS

Honor your wife. Any husband who doesn't honor his Creator first and wife second is destined for problems, and soon.

YOUR OWN IDEAS ABOUT . . .
The Importance of Establishing Sensible Priorities.

_____

_____

_____

_____

_____

_____

_____

_____

_____

_____

_____

_____

_____

_____

_____

_____

_____

_____

26

What Every Husband Should Say to His Wife:

"I UNDERSTAND THE IMPORTANCE OF CLEAR, LOVING, OPEN LINES OF COMMUNICATION."

A word fitly spoken is like apples of gold in settings of silver.

Proverbs 25:11 NKJV

Your skills as a communicator will have a profound impact upon your relationships, starting with that most important relationship: your marriage. Here are a few simple rules that can help: 1. Think First, Speak Second: If you blurt out the first thing that comes into your head, you may say things that are better left unsaid. 2. Learn to Be a Good Listener: Far too many marriages are unsuccessful because one or both spouses simply don't make the effort to listen. If you want your marriage to flourish, listen carefully to your spouse. 3. Don't Be a Chronic Complainer: You'll never whine your way to a happy marriage, so don't even try. 4. Be a Trustworthy Communicator: Don't hedge the truth, don't omit important facts, and don't make promises that you can't keep. 5. Be Encouraging: You should be your spouse's biggest booster, not your spouse's constant critic.

God's Word reminds us that "Reckless words pierce like a sword, but the tongue of the wise brings healing" (Proverbs 12:18 NIV). So, if you seek to be a source of encouragement to your loved ones, you must measure your words carefully. You must speak wisely, not impulsively. You must use words of kindness and praise, not words of anger or derision. And, you must learn how to be truthful without being cruel.

You have the power to lift your loved ones up or to hold them back. When you learn how to lift them up, you'll soon discover that you've lifted yourself up, too.

More from God's Word About Communication

The heart of the wise teaches his mouth, and adds learning to his lips.

Proverbs 16:23 NKJV

An ungodly man digs up evil, and it is on his lips like a burning fire.

Proverbs 16:27 NKJV

May the words of my mouth and the meditation of my heart be acceptable to You, Lord, my rock and my Redeemer.

Psalm 19:14 HCSB

Nevertheless let each one of you in particular so love his own wife as himself . . . .

Ephesians 5:33 NKJV

But I say unto you, That every idle word that men shall speak, they shall give account thereof in the day of judgment. For by thy words thou shalt be justified, and by thy words thou shalt be condemned.

Matthew 12:36-37 KJV

MORE GREAT IDEAS . . .

How much of our lives are, well, so daily. How often our hours are filled with the mundane, seemingly unimportant things that have to be done, whether at home or work. These very "daily" tasks could become a celebration of praise. "It is through consecration," someone has said, "that drudgery is made divine."

Gigi Graham Tchividjian

Some of us seem so anxious about avoiding hell that we forget to celebrate our journey toward heaven.

Philip Yancey

God has a course mapped out for your life, and all the inadequacies in the world will not change His mind. He will be with you every step of the way. And though it may take time, He has a celebration planned for when you cross over the "Red Seas" of your life.

Charles Swindoll

Part of good communication is listening with the eyes as well as with the ears.

Josh McDowell

The main joy of heaven will be the heavenly Father greeting us in a time and place of rejoicing, celebration, joy, and great reunion.

Bill Bright

In terms of the parable of the Prodigal Son, repentance is the flight home that leads to joyful celebration. It opens the way to a future, to a relationship restored.

Philip Yancey

Both a good marriage and a bad marriage have moments of struggle, but in a healthy relationship, the husband and wife search for answers and areas of agreement because they love each other.

James Dobson

A TIP FOR HUSBANDS

Communication is vital to the health of any marriage. If you're having trouble expressing yourself, don't clam up. Instead, keep trying until you finally get the hang of it.

YOUR OWN IDEAS ABOUT . . .
The Importance of Effective Communication
Within Your Marriage.

_____

_____

_____

_____

_____

_____

_____

_____

_____

_____

_____

_____

_____

_____

_____

_____

27

What Every Husband Should Say to His Wife:

"I THANK YOU FOR YOUR PRAYERS, AND I WILL NEVER STOP PRAYING FOR YOU."

The intense prayer of the righteous is very powerful.
James 5:16 HCSB

Is prayer an integral part of your married life, or is it a hit-or-miss habit? Do you and your wife "pray without ceasing," or is prayer usually an afterthought? Do you regularly pray together, or do you only bow your heads in unison during Sunday morning services? The answers to these questions determine the quality of your prayer life and, to a surprising extent, the spiritual strength of your marriage.

Andrew Murray observed, "Some people pray just to pray, and some people pray to know God." Your task, along with your wife, is to pray together, not out of habit or obligation, but out of a sincere desire to know your Heavenly Father.

Through constant prayers, you and your bride should petition God, you should praise God, and you should seek God's guidance for your marriage and your life.

Prayer changes things, prayer changes people, and prayer changes marriages. So don't limit your prayers to meals or to bedtime. Pray constantly about things great and small. God is listening, and He wants to hear from you—and your spouse—right now.

MORE FROM GOD'S WORD ABOUT PRAYER

If you really carry out the royal law prescribed in Scripture, You shall love your neighbor as yourself, you are doing well.

James 2:8 HCSB

Therefore I want the men in every place to pray, lifting up holy hands without anger or argument.

1 Timothy 2:8 HCSB

And let us not grow weary while doing good, for in due season we shall reap if we do not lose heart.

Galatians 6:9 NKJV

And whenever you stand praying, if you have anything against anyone, forgive him, that your Father in heaven may also forgive you your trespasses.

Mark 11:25 NKJV

Rejoice in hope; be patient in affliction; be persistent in prayer.

Romans 12:12 HCSB

MORE FROM GOD'S WORD ABOUT SILENCE

Be still, and know that I am God.

Psalm 46:10 NKJV

Be silent before the Lord and wait expectantly for Him.

Psalm 37:7 HCSB

In quietness and confidence shall be your strength.

Isaiah 30:15 NKJV

I am not alone, because the Father is with Me.

John 16:32 HCSB

Draw near to God, and He will draw near to you.

James 4:8 HCSB

More Great Ideas . . .

The hard part about being a praying wife is maintaining a pure heart. If you have resentment, anger, unforgiveness, or an ungodly attitude—even if there's good reason for it—you'll have a difficult time seeing answers to your prayers. But if you can release those feelings to God in total honesty, there is nothing that can change a marriage more dramatically.

Stormie Omartian

As we join together in prayer, we draw on God's enabling might in a way that multiplies our own efforts many times over.

Shirley Dobson

Our prayer must not be self-centered. It must arise not only because we feel our own need as a burden we must lay upon God, but also because we are so bound up in love for our fellow men that we feel their needs as acutely as our own. To make intercession for men is the most powerful and practical way in which we can express our love for them.

John Calvin

In souls filled with love, the desire to please God is continual prayer.

John Wesley

We must lay before Him what is in us, not what ought to be in us.

C. S. Lewis

Jesus practiced secret prayer and asked us to follow His example.

Catherine Marshall

A TIP FOR HUSBANDS

Today, think about your family's prayer life. Are you really in touch with God? If so, keep it up; if not, talk to your spouse about the need to carve out more time with God.

Your Own Ideas About . . .
The Importance of Prayer.

_____

_____

_____

_____

_____

_____

_____

_____

_____

_____

_____

_____

_____

_____

_____

_____

_____

_____

28

What Every Husband Should Say to His Wife:

"YOU ARE MY BEST FRIEND."

A man leaves his father and mother and bonds with his wife,
and they become one flesh.

Genesis 2:24 HCSB

Do you want your love to last forever? If so, here's a time-tested prescription for a blissfully happy marriage: make certain that your spouse is your best friend.

Genuine friendship between a husband and wife should be treasured and nurtured. As Christians, we are commanded to love one another. The familiar words of 1 Corinthians 13:2 remind us that love and charity are among God's greatest gifts: "And though I have the gift of prophecy, and understand all mysteries, and all knowledge; and though I have all faith, so that I could remove mountains, and have not charity, I am nothing" (KJV).

Is your bride your best friend? If so, you are immensely blessed by God—never take this gift for granted. So today, remember the important role that friendship plays in your marriage. That friendship is, after all, a glorious gift, praised by God. Give thanks for that gift and nurture it.

MORE FROM GOD'S WORD ABOUT FRIENDSHIP

I give thanks to my God for every remembrance of you.

Philippians 1:3 HCSB

Beloved, if God so loved us, we also ought to love one another.

1 John 4:11 NKJV

A friend loves at all times . . . .

Proverbs 17:17 HCSB

Love one another earnestly from a pure heart.

1 Peter 1:22 HCSB

Oil and incense bring joy to the heart, and the sweetness of a friend is better than self-counsel.

Proverbs 27:9 HCSB

More Great Ideas . . .

On the pleasant days of marriage, gaze across at your groom and conclude he is worth it. On the difficult days of marriage, gaze up at your Groom and conclude He's worth it.

Beth Moore

How much a person loves someone is obvious by how much he is willing to sacrifice for that person.

Bill Bright

How do you spell love? When you reach the point where the happiness, security, and development of another person is as much of a driving force to you as your own happiness, security, and development, then you have a mature love. True love is spelled G-I-V-E. It is not based on what you can get, but rooted in what you can give to the other person.

Josh McDowell

Affection is responsible for nine-tenths of whatever solid and durable happiness there is in our natural lives.

C. S. Lewis

The Holy Spirit was given to guide us into all truth, but He doesn't do it all at once.

Elisabeth Elliot

The best evidence of our having the truth is our walking in the truth.

Matthew Henry

Having a doctrine pass before the mind is not what the Bible means by knowing the truth. It's only when it reaches down deep into the heart that the truth begins to set us free, just as a key must penetrate a lock to turn it, or as rainfall must saturate the earth down to the roots in order for your garden to grow.

John Eldredge

A TIP FOR HUSBANDS

It takes time to build a friendship . . . including the friendship with your wife. So take the time, and make the time, to be best friends.

YOUR OWN IDEAS ABOUT . . .
Ways You and Your Wife Can Continue
to Be Best Friends.

_____

_____

_____

_____

_____

_____

_____

_____

_____

_____

_____

_____

_____

_____

_____

29

What Every Husband Should Say to His Wife:

"I Thank God for Our Marriage."

*He who finds a wife finds what is good
and receives favor from the Lord.*
Proverbs 18:22 NIV

Your life and your marriage are gifts from God: celebrate those blessings and give thanks. And make no mistake: When you celebrate the gifts of life and love, your thankful heart will serve as a powerful blessing to your bride.

Every good gift comes from God. As believers who have been saved by a risen Christ, we owe unending thanksgiving to our Heavenly Father. Yet sometimes, amid the crush of everyday living, we simply don't stop long enough to pause and thank our Creator for His countless blessings. As Christians, we are blessed beyond measure. Thus, thanksgiving should become a habit, a regular part of our daily routines.

Thoughtful believers can face the inevitable challenges of married life armed with the joy of Christ and the promise of salvation. So whatever this day holds for you, begin it and end it with God as your partner and Christ as your Savior. And throughout the day, give thanks to the One who created you and saved you. Place God squarely at the center of your marriage and your life. Then celebrate! God's love for you is infinite. Accept it joyously and be thankful.

MORE FROM GOD'S WORD ABOUT THANKSGIVING

Give thanks to the Lord, for He is good; His faithful love endures forever.

Psalm 118:29 HCSB

I will give You thanks with all my heart.

Psalm 138:1 HCSB

And whatever you do, in word or in deed, do everything in the name of the Lord Jesus, giving thanks to God the Father through Him.

Colossians 3:17 HCSB

Therefore as you have received Christ Jesus the Lord, walk in Him, rooted and built up in Him and established in the faith, just as you were taught, and overflowing with thankfulness.

Colossians 2:6-7 HCSB

Thanks be to God for His indescribable gift.

2 Corinthians 9:15 HCSB

MORE FROM GOD'S WORD ABOUT WORSHIP

And every day they devoted themselves to meeting together in the temple complex, and broke bread from house to house. They ate their food with gladness and simplicity of heart, praising God and having favor with all the people. And every day the Lord added those being saved to them.

Acts 2:46-47 HCSB

But an hour is coming, and is now here, when the true worshipers will worship the Father in spirit and truth. Yes, the Father wants such people to worship Him. God is Spirit, and those who worship Him must worship in spirit and truth.

John 4:23-24 HCSB

For where two or three are gathered together in My name, I am there among them.

Matthew 18:20 HCSB

So that at the name of Jesus every knee should bow—of those who are in heaven and on earth and under the earth—and every tongue should confess that Jesus Christ is Lord, to the glory of God the Father.

Philippians 2:10-11 HCSB

MORE GREAT IDEAS . . .

God has promised that if we harvest well with the tools of thanksgiving, there will be seeds for planting in the spring.

Gloria Gaither

It is always possible to be thankful for what is given rather than to complain about what is not given. One or the other becomes a habit of life.

Elisabeth Elliot

A friend is one who makes me do my best.

Oswald Chambers

The joy of the Holy Spirit is experienced by giving thanks in all situations.

Bill Bright

Thank God every morning when you get up that you have something to do that day which must be done, whether you like it or not.

Charles Kingsley

Praise and thank God for who He is and for what He has done for you.

Billy Graham

The words "thank" and "think" come from the same root word. If we would think more, we would thank more.

Warren Wiersbe

God often keeps us on the path by guiding us through the counsel of friends and trusted spiritual advisors.

Bill Hybels

A TIP FOR HUSBANDS

Since you're thankful to God, tell Him so. And keep telling Him so every day of your life.

YOUR OWN IDEAS ABOUT . . .

Some of the Reasons You're Thankful for Your Marriage.

_____

_____

_____

_____

_____

_____

_____

_____

_____

_____

_____

_____

_____

_____

_____

_____

_____

_____

30

What Every Husband
Should Say to His Wife:

"OUR LOVE WILL LAST FOREVER."

Love never ends.

1 Corinthians 13:8 HCSB

The Bible makes it clear that God's love for you and your wife is deeper and more profound than either of you can imagine.

When you and your spouse embrace God together, both of you are forever changed. When you embrace God's love, you feel differently about yourself, your marriage, your family, and your world. When you join together and accept God's love, the two of you will be transformed.

God loved this world so much that He sent His Son to save it. And now only one real question remains: what will you and your wife do in response to God's love? The answer should be obvious: If you haven't already done so, accept Jesus Christ as your Savior. He's waiting patiently for you, but please don't make Him wait another minute longer.

So, if you and your wife genuinely want to build a love that endures, make God the focus of your marriage. When you do, your marriage will last forever—and so will your love.

MORE FROM GOD'S WORD ABOUT ETERNAL LIFE

For God loved the world in this way: He gave His only Son, so that everyone who believes in Him will not perish but have eternal life.

John 3:16 HCSB

And this is the testimony: God has given us eternal life, and this life is in His Son. The one who has the Son has life. The one who doesn't have the Son of God does not have life.

1 John 5:11-12 HCSB

Pursue righteousness, godliness, faith, love, endurance, and gentleness. Fight the good fight for the faith; take hold of eternal life, to which you were called and have made a good confession before many witnesses.

1 Timothy 6:11-12 HCSB

Jesus said to her, "I am the resurrection and the life. The one who believes in Me, even if he dies, will live. Everyone who lives and believes in Me will never die—ever. Do you believe this?"

John 11:25-26 HCSB

MORE FROM GOD'S WORD ABOUT GOD'S LOVE

For the Lord is good, and His love is eternal; His faithfulness endures through all generations.

Psalm 100:5 HCSB

[Because of] the Lord's faithful love we do not perish, for His mercies never end. They are new every morning; great is Your faithfulness!

Lamentations 3:22-23 HCSB

Help me, Lord my God; save me according to Your faithful love.

Psalm 109:26 HCSB

What a gift life is to those who stay the course! You've heard, of course, of Job's staying power, and you know how God brought it all together for him at the end. That's because God cares, cares right down to the last detail.

James 5:11 MSG

More Great Ideas . . .

Love simply cannot spring up without that self-surrender to each other. If either withholds the self, love cannot exist.

E. Stanley Jones

Life without love is empty and meaningless no matter how gifted we are.

Charles Stanley

To have fallen in love hints to our hearts that all of earthly life is not hopelessly fallen. Love is the laughter of God.

Beth Moore

The whole being of any Christian is Faith and Love. Faith brings the man to God; love brings him to men.

Martin Luther

Life is immortal, love eternal; death is nothing but a horizon, and a horizon is only the limit of our vision.

Corrie ten Boom

If you are a believer, your judgment will not determine your eternal destiny. Christ's finished work on Calvary was applied to you the moment you accepted Christ as Savior.

Beth Moore

I can still hardly believe it. I, with shriveled, bent fingers, atrophied muscles, gnarled knees, and no feeling from the shoulders down, will one day have a new body—light, bright and clothed in righteousness—powerful and dazzling.

Joni Eareckson Tada

Once a man is united to God, how could he not live forever? Once a man is separated from God, what can he do but wither and die?

C. S. Lewis

A TIP FOR HUSBANDS

The ultimate choice is your choice to welcome God's Son into your heart and by doing so accept the gift of eternal life. If you or your wife haven't already done so, make that choice today.

YOUR OWN IDEAS ABOUT . . .
What the Gift of Eternal Life Means to You
and Your Wife.

_____

_____

_____

_____

_____

_____

_____

_____

_____

_____

_____

_____

_____

_____

_____

_____